DATE DUE

N

The Loch Ness Monster

A photograph by P. A. MacNab of West Kilbride, Scotland. It is the only picture of Nessie that shows her size in relation to objects on the shore. (Copyright P. A. MacNab)

The
Loch Ness
Monster

by Elwood D. Baumann

FRANKLIN WATTS | NEW YORK | LONDON

To Christie and Jeff Baumann

SBN: 531-02031-2
Library of Congress Catalog Card Number: 72-182896
Printed in the United States of America
9   8

The Loch Ness Monster

SCOTLAND

0   50
Scale of Miles

ORKNEY ISLANDS

John o'Groat's

Thurso

Wick

*NORT.
SEA*

Isle of
Lewis

North Minch

Dornoch

Braemore

*Moray
Firth*

Elgin   Banff

Nairn

Peterl

NORTHWEST HIGHLANDS

Inverness

Loch Ness

**LOCH NESS AREA
OF INVERNESS**

Isle of
Skye

Fort
Augustus

Caledonian Canal

Aberdeen

□Balmoral
Castle

HIGHLANDS

Fort
William

△*Ben Nevis
4406 ft.*

GRAMPIAN MOUNTAINS

Montros

HIGHLANDS

INNER HEBRIDES

Mull I.

Firth of Lorne

Oban

Dundee

Firth of Tay

Perth   St. Andrews

Kinross

*Loch
Lomond*

Stirling

Firth of Forth

Jura I.

Dunbarton

Falkirk   Dunbar

Greenock

Clydebank

Paisley

■**GLASGOW**

■**EDINBURGH**

Sound of Jura

Islay I.

Motherwell

L O W L A N D S

Berwick
-on-
Tweed

Arran I.

*Firth
of
Clyde*

Kilmarnock

Lanark

Peebles

Campbeltown

Ayr

Prestwick

Selkirk

*CHEVIOT
HILLS*

SOUTHERN UPLANDS

NORTHERN

North Channel

Stranraer

Dumfries

IRELAND

*Solway
Firth*

ENGLAN

Chapter 1

There are many people in the Scottish Highlands who still speak the ancient Gaelic language. *Loch* is the Gaelic word for "lake." Until quite recent times, Loch Ness was known as *Loch na Beiste*. The Lake of the Monster.

Loch Ness is a rather frightening place. The water is full of peat particles and is inky black. Sudden storms lash the loch. Going out in a small boat can be very dangerous; no one in his right mind would swim there.

It's twenty-four miles from one end of the loch to the other, but it's only two miles across at its widest point. The average depth is about seven hundred feet. There are very few beaches and none of them are very large. In most places, the banks plunge straight down into the dark depths.

The country surrounding Loch Ness is wildly beautiful. Herds of deer live in the pine forests and there are wild goats on the rocky crags. Patches of snow can often be seen on the hilltops until July or August. Snow falling close to the loch, however, usually melts within a few hours. The loch never freezes and the great volume of relatively warm water helps to keep the climate mild. Although Loch Ness is in the same latitude as Moscow, the winter weather is quite pleasant.

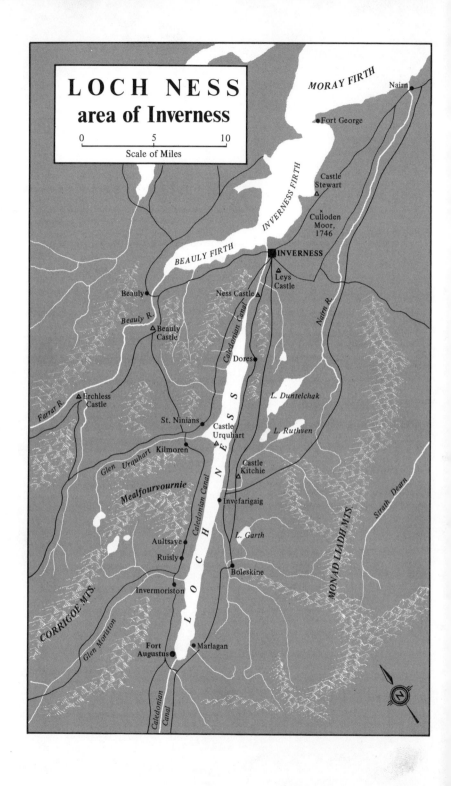

LOCH NESS
area of Inverness

0   5   10

Scale of Miles

MORAY FIRTH

Nairn

Fort George

Castle Stewart

INVERNESS FIRTH

Culloden Moor, 1746

BEAULY FIRTH

INVERNESS

Leys Castle

Beauly

Ness Castle

Caledonian Canal

Beauly R.

Beauly Castle

Dores

Nairn R.

L. Duntelchak

Erchless Castle

Farrar R.

St. Ninians

L. Ruthven

Castle Urquhart

Glen Urquhart

Kilmoren

Castle Kitchie

Mealfourvournie

Invefarigaig

L. Garth

Caledonian Canal

Aultsaye

Ruisly

L O C H   N E S S

Strath Dearn

MONADH LIADH MTS.

Boleskine

Invermoriston

CORRIGOE MTS.

Glen Moriston

Fort Augustus

Marlagan

Caledonian Canal

N

The Ness Valley is sparsely populated. Most of the men are either sheep farmers or foresters. They are friendly hardworking people who really don't care very much about things that happen outside their valley. Everything they need can be bought in the tiny villages scattered on both sides of the loch. The names of the villages remind visitors that this was once a Gaelic-speaking area. Many people find names like Drumnadrochit, Clachnaharry, Achnahannet, and Inverfarigaig almost impossible to pronounce.

When summer comes, visitors from all parts of the world pour into the Scottish Highlands. Some of them want to explore the ancient castles of kings and dukes. Others are there to fish trout and salmon. Some have come to camp out in the forests or to pitch a tent near one of the innumerable streams and lochs. Still others have come to enjoy the spectacular beauty of northern Scotland.

The Scottish Highlands have many attractions, and people visit them for many different reasons. There is one very special attraction, however, that brings many thousands of visitors to Loch Ness each summer.

That attraction is the world-famous Loch Ness Monster.

Chapter 2

It was in the summer of 1933 that a strange story came out of the Scottish Highlands. The story said that an enormous monster had been seen in Loch Ness. Radio announcers and newspapermen were delighted. This was the sort of news they liked to get. They knew that everyone was interested in monsters.

They were right. Everyone *was* interested in monsters, but very few people believed that they actually existed. The Age of Monsters had ended millions of years ago. It simply wasn't possible that there was one still alive and going strong. Besides, what would a monster be doing in a freshwater loch in the Scottish Highlands? The story was just too ridiculous to be true.

The story may have sounded ridiculous, but it refused to die. More and more people reported seeing a monster in Loch Ness. These people weren't crackpots, either. They were sincere and reliable folks who were honestly reporting what they had seen.

Scientists scoffed at the reports. They knew that many of the Highlanders were deeply superstitious people. Life was lonely in their remote valley and they often let their imaginations run wild. Then, too, the Highlanders drank a great deal of the Scotch whisky they made in their own stills. It was probably after a few glasses of whisky that they saw the monster.

To the scientists, the monster presented no problem at all. It was not possible for a monster to be in Loch Ness, they reasoned; therefore, there *was* no monster in Loch Ness. To millions of other people in the world, the Loch Ness Monster became a huge joke.

But the people in the lonely Scottish Highlands weren't laughing. Many of them had seen the monster, so how could anyone tell them that the monster did not exist?

The sudden rash of sightings was one of the many things that puzzled the outside world. Why was it, they wondered, that all of a sudden dozens of people were seeing the monster? Why hadn't anyone seen it before?

This can easily be explained. The Highlanders had always known that there was "a horrible great beastie" in Loch Ness. It had been seen on many different occasions by many different people. One old man remembers his mother telling him to stay away from the loch or the "terrible water kelpie" would get him.

Although the Highlanders are wonderfully friendly people, they're inclined to be a bit suspicious of strangers. This was much more the case thirty or forty years ago than it is now. At the time that the Loch Ness Monster first made world headlines, very few people visited this remote region. If they did hear about the monster, or if they did happen to see it, they didn't report the fact to the press or radio.

Chances of seeing the monster were, of course, extremely unlikely. The chances of hearing about it weren't much better. Even today the Highlanders are rather reluctant to discuss the Loch Ness Monster with an outsider.

The reason for the sudden rash of sightings can also be explained easily. In the spring of 1933, it was decided to build a road along the northern shore of the loch. Until that time, there had been only a very narrow path winding through the pine forest. The loch was seldom in sight.

Hundreds of men were employed on the road-building project. The course of the road ran close to the loch for most of its length. Trees were felled and workers had a clear view of the water.

This is rugged country and the engineers frequently had to blast their way through solid rock. Countless tons of it rumbled down the hillside and splashed into the loch. Scientists now know that Nessie, as everyone calls the monster, is very sensitive to noise. The slam of a car door or an excited shout will cause her to sink out of sight immediately.

Some scientists think that the blasting and rumbling may have disturbed Nessie and she came up to see what was going on. Whether that is the case or not is hard to say. One thing, however, is certain. While the road was being built, there were more people observing the loch than ever before. It's not surprising, then, that the number of sightings suddenly increased dramatically.

One of the sightings was particularly dramatic. It was so dramatic, in fact, that it was difficult to believe at the time. Fortunately, the witnesses were reliable and completely sensible people.

The startling incident occurred in July of 1933. Mr. and Mrs. George Spicer of London were driving slowly along the southern shore of the loch. It was the middle of a bright and sunny day. Visibility was perfect. Suddenly Mrs. Spicer jerked bolt upright. "What in the world is that?" she cried out in alarm.

The two people in the car could hardly believe what they

were seeing. Some type of enormous animal was crossing the road in front of them. They saw first what appeared to be a massive elephant's trunk stretching all the way across the road. Not until a huge body came out of the bushes did they realize that the trunklike affair was the creature's neck.

George Spicer and his wife stared in amazement as the animal lurched ponderously toward the loch. There was a slight rise between the monster and Spicer's car and the lower part of the creature could not be seen. It was impossible to tell whether it had legs or flippers or what. The loch at this point was less than twenty yards from the road. While the Spicers stared, the creature descended the slope and disappeared into the water.

Scientists who interviewed Mr. and Mrs. Spicer were convinced that they had seen something most unusual. But what? There were no more monsters left in the world, so what had they seen?

George Spicer described the creature as an abomination. "It looked sort of like a giant snail with a long neck," he told the men who interviewed him. "It was a loathsome thing," said Mrs. Spicer. "It was simply horrible."

The men of science studied the sketch George Spicer had drawn of the creature he had seen. It showed a long, undulating neck and a huge rounded body. There was no sign of a tail. Spicer, however, had seen a strange fleshy object sticking up at the point where the monster's neck joined the body. He believed that this was the tip of the tail. It had been curved around and alongside the body while the creature was lurching through the bushes.

There could be no doubt but that the Spicers were completely sincere. The husband was the managing director of a large company in London. His wife was an honest and intelligent woman. Both of them were willing to make sworn statements that they were telling the truth and accurately describing what they had seen.

The story and the sketch interested the scientists very much. Their conclusions, however, were a disappointment. They openly declared that the creature the Spicers claimed to have seen did not exist because it could not exist. A monster that lived in a freshwater lake and strolled around on forested hillsides was just too much to be true.

Bertram Mills, owner of Mills' Circus, apparently thought so too. He offered a reward of one hundred thousand dollars to the man who brought him the Loch Ness Monster.

Chapter 3

Four months after the Spicers' startling experience, a Highlander named Hugh Gray was strolling leisurely along a narrow footpath near the village of Foyers. It was a beautiful day. The sun was shining brightly; the loch was as calm as a mirror.

While Gray was admiring the view, the calm surface of the loch was disturbed by a violent commotion. There was a sudden upheaval of water. A great rounded back rose up from the depths and a powerful tail began lashing the water. Spray flew in all directions. Mr. Gray couldn't see the creature's head, but he estimated the length of the tail and body to be forty feet long. He was truly seeing a monster.

It's highly unusual for a Highlander to carry a camera, but Hugh Gray had fortunately brought his with him that morning. The monster was thrashing about approximately a hundred yards away. Although spray was flying thick and fast, Gray raised his camera and snapped five pictures before the creature submerged.

11

Hugh Gray's photograph, the first ever taken of the Loch Ness Monster. (Copyright Scottish Daily Record and Sunday Mail*)*

Four of the five pictures were complete blanks. The fifth one was by no means good. Gray had used a cheap box camera. Light had somehow entered it and the fifth photograph had been partially damaged. It did, however, show that there was some sort of large creature in the loch. At last the world had a picture of the famous Loch Ness Monster.

People reacted to the photograph in many ways. Some

12

were finally convinced that an unusually large animal lived in the loch. Others didn't know what to think, and a few others simply scoffed. The chief scoffer was a professor of zoology at Glasgow University. After a quick glance at the photograph, he declared, "It's absurd to suppose that a monster can exist in Loch Ness."

Not everyone agreed. Scientists at the British Museum stated that it *might* be a bottle-nosed whale or one of the larger species of sharks.

A bit more interest was aroused at Manchester University. The zoologists there were inclined to think that the creature was a rorqual, which is a member of the whale family. Then a closer examination of the photograph under a powerful magnifying glass revealed something no one else had noticed. There were two smooth, oval-shaped objects growing from the side of the creature's body. One was toward the front of the torso; the other was toward the rear. The objects rather resembled paddles, or flippers.

The scientists scratched their heads. Rorquals didn't have rear flippers, or paddles. It followed, therefore, that the object in the photograph could not possibly be a rorqual. So what was it then? they asked one another. Nobody knew the answer to that one and the problem remained unsolved. One zoologist even reported to the press that the photograph was probably not of a living creature.

Scientists were still puzzling over Hugh Gray's photograph when three men arrived at Loch Ness. One of them was Mr. F.W. Memory, an associate editor of one of England's largest daily newspapers. His two companions were a big-game hunter and a photographer. Memory hoped to gather enough material to write a sensational story on the Loch Ness Monster. He got his story all right and it was a truly sensational one.

13

For the first few days, the hunter and the photographer chugged up and down the loch in a motorboat. On the fourth evening they rushed back to camp in a state of high excitement. They had found the tracks of a monster on the shore of the loch. There were several complete footmarks clearly showing four toes and a large pad.

Mr. Memory was skeptical. He knew that Highlanders had often searched the shores of the loch hoping to find some sign of the monster. How did it happen then that the hunter had found them in only four days? Was it simply good luck or was the man telling a story?

The hunter had a ready answer. He explained that he had spent many years hunting big game in Africa. The habits of large animals were familiar to him. He knew where they were likely to be found, so he'd had no trouble finding the tracks.

It seemed like a logical story and Memory swallowed it. Rushing into Inverness, he phoned his paper and gave them the exciting news. International wire services picked up the story at once. Millions of people throughout the world were thrilled to hear that tracks of the Loch Ness Monster had been found. Perhaps now scientists could discover what sort of a creature inhabited the loch's dark depths.

Bright and early the next morning, the big-game hunter and the photographer set out to make a plaster cast of the monster's tracks. For reasons known only to themselves, they refused to let any of the local residents see their handiwork. The cast was crated carefully and shipped to the British Museum to be identified.

That night the hunter broadcast a dramatic speech to a radio audience of millions. The Loch Ness Monster, he told them, was an enormous amphibian of some prehistoric type.

14

It might be as much as a hundred feet long. How many tons it might weigh would be a difficult thing to guess. The hunter admitted that he was not a zoologist, but his personal belief was that the Loch Ness Monster was a type of seagoing dinosaur.

Several scientists thought he might just possibly be right.

Chapter **4**

While the plaster cast was being studied at the British Museum, some utterly fantastic things were happening at Loch Ness.

Mr. T. P. Grant, a native Highlander who had lived all his life on the loch, was returning home from Inverness on his motorcycle. Although it was late at night, the entire landscape was bathed in bright moonlight. Visibility was no problem.

As Grant was approaching the village of Abriachan, he noticed a large, dark object on the side of the road. Getting off his motorcycle, he moved cautiously forward. It was light enough for him to see that an animal with a head rather like that of a snake or an eel was watching him.

Grant was less than twenty yards from the creature when it burst out of the shadow of the bushes. It bounded swiftly away from him, charged through the undergrowth on the opposite side of the road, and plunged down into the loch with a mighty splash.

Fortunately, Grant was a keen observer, a student of natural history, and a practical man. After carefully marking the spot where the beast had entered the loch, he hurried on to his

16

brother's house in Drumnadrochit. There he drew a detailed sketch and wrote out a complete report of what he had seen. It was beyond a doubt the best description anyone had ever been able to provide.

According to Grant's sketch and report, the animal's small head was flat on top. It had a long neck and a long, powerful tail. The body was massive, the rear quarters being considerably larger than the front. When crossing the road, it had bounded rather like a kangaroo. There were four limbs. The front ones were comparatively small. The pair in back were considerably larger. Grant estimated the total length of the animal to be approximately twenty feet.

The first thing Grant did the following morning was to return to the place where the monster had entered the water. There was almost nothing to be seen. Only a trail of flattened grass marked the creature's path.

Word that Grant had seen the Loch Ness Monster on land and had observed it at close range spread swiftly from one end of the loch to the other. People were surprised, but they had no reason to doubt the story. Grant was a professional man of absolute integrity. He was highly regarded by everyone who knew him. Others may play games with the truth, but not Grant. If he said that he had seen the monster on land, then he had very definitely seen the monster on land.

One of those who heard the story was the hunter who had made a plaster cast of the monster's tracks. For personal reasons, he decided to visit the place where the incident had occurred. This wasn't difficult to arrange. A few discreet inquiries in Drumnadrochit gave him all the information he needed.

Mr. Memory, the newspaperman, was delighted with the way things were going. The whole world was interested in the Loch Ness Monster and he had been able to give the reading

17

public some exciting news. First his little expedition had found the monster's tracks. Now he had the testimony of a man who had seen the creature on land. Mr. Memory decided that one more thing was needed: a photograph of the eyewitness at the place where the monster had plunged into the loch.

Grant explained to Memory that the only signs of the monster's path were some patches of flattened grass. There was nothing else to be seen. Nevertheless, he reluctantly agreed to accompany Mr. Memory, the big-game hunter, and the photographer to the spot where he had seen the creature.

A tremendous surprise awaited Grant. After showing the three men where the monster had been standing, he led them down the slope to the loch. To his absolute amazement, a pile of bones and part of the carcass of a goat lay at the water's edge. But there was more than that! Clearly defined footmarks of some giant creature were all over the place.

It was impossible for poor Mr. Grant to know what to think. He had examined the area closely only a few hours earlier. At that time he had seen nothing at all unusual. A few patches of flattened grass were the only sign that a large animal had come down the side of the loch. What in the world was going on? he asked himself. How had the tracks and the pile of bones and the dead goat gotten there? What was this all about, anyway? he wondered.

Although he suspected some sort of a hoax, the large footmarks intrigued Grant. Getting down on his hands and knees, he inspected them closely. Each track clearly showed four toes and a large pad. Being a student of natural history, Grant noticed that the tracks were very similar to those of a hippopotamus.

The big-game hunter agreed. He had noticed the same thing, he said. The tracks he had found of the Loch Ness

18

Monster closely resembled the hippopotamus tracks he had seen when hunting in Africa.

The unfortunate Grant was more confused than ever. He knew perfectly well that the creature he had seen the night before had not been a hippopotamus. The pile of bones and the dead goat only deepened the mystery. Hippos were vegetarians. They never ate meat, so some other creature was responsible for the dead goat and the bones.

But what kind of a creature? Mr. Grant couldn't answer that question. He was absolutely convinced, however, that the Loch Ness Monster was not a hippopotamus.

Chapter 5

On the same day that the four men examined the strange signs on the shores of the loch, zoologists at the British Museum issued a report to the press.

They had concluded their examination of the plaster cast of the footmark of the Loch Ness Monster, they announced.

All of them had agreed that the plaster cast bore a marked similarity to the footmark of a hippopotamus. There was a mounted hippo in the museum and a plaster cast had been made of the foot. The resemblance between the two casts was striking.

To be absolutely certain, however, the scientists went to the London Zoo and made a cast of the foot of a live female hippo. It proved to be almost identical with the cast sent to them by the big-game hunter at Loch Ness.

Their conclusions left no room for doubt. The plaster cast said to be the footmark of the Loch Ness Monster had actually been made from the right hind foot of a nearly full-grown hippopotamus.

The unfortunate hoax had far-reaching effects. The hunter, the man who had caused all the trouble, put the hippo foot into his suitcase and left Loch Ness in a hurry. Mr. F. W. Memory, the man who had hired the hunter, almost died of embarrassment. He had been completely taken in by the hoax. Because he had believed the hunter's stories, he had phoned them to his newspaper office. As a result, millions of innocent people had also been deceived.

Scientists chuckled at the hoax and looked wise. They had always scoffed at the idea of a monster in a freshwater lake. Others, too, were vastly amused. They had never believed in the Loch Ness Monster. It had been nothing but a huge joke to them. Now it appeared that they had been right all the time.

Not everyone, of course, was laughing. The hunter's hoax put many folks into a most embarrassing situation. Those who claimed to have seen the Loch Ness Monster were sometimes made objects of ridicule. People laughed at them and believed that they were a bit soft in the head.

This was unfortunate in more ways than one. The Highlanders had never liked to discuss the monster with outsiders. They knew that some people looked upon it as a joke and they didn't want to make themselves appear ridiculous. The hunter's hoax made them more close mouthed than ever.

There are very few people today who doubt the existence of a huge unidentified creature in Loch Ness. Scientific expeditions have tracked it with sophisticated electronic equipment. Many hundreds of people have seen it. Nevertheless, the Highlanders still try to steer clear of any discussion of the monster. Many sightings are never officially reported.

There is one outstanding example of this. The sighting occurred nearly twenty years ago, but came to light only recently.

A resident of Drumnadrochit came into the pub late one evening. His face was ashen. His hands were trembling so badly that he was barely able to get his glass of whisky up to his mouth. It was obvious to everyone that the man had undergone some sort of frightening experience, but he refused to talk about it.

Seeing the condition the man was in, the bartender offered him a ride home. When they arrived, the man reluctantly agreed to tell the bartender what had happened to him. First, however, he made him promise not to repeat the story to anyone until after his death. The bartender promised and the man told his story.

He had gone out in the afternoon to fish for salmon. It was a warm day and he drifted along lazily in his small boat. Without any warning whatsoever, an enormous and hideous creature suddenly burst up from the depths. Less than ten feet separated the monster from the man. A cry of terror caught in the man's throat. He leaped to his feet, then pitched headlong to the bottom of the boat. When he regained consciousness, there was no sign of the fearful monster that had frightened him out of his wits.

The bartender kept his promise for nearly twenty years. No one was told the story until after the man's death.

Chapter **6**

People were still chuckling over the hunter's hippo foot hoax when Nessie again made world headlines.

Dr. H. K. Wilson, a London surgeon and an amateur naturalist, was driving along the loch very early one morning. Like everyone else who motors alongside Loch Ness, he was keeping an eye out for the monster.

And then he saw it! Or at least he saw something. Stopping the car, he grabbed his camera and telephoto lens. There was definitely a commotion going on about two hundred yards from the shore. While the doctor watched, a head and neck rose up from the water. Dr. Wilson swiftly made the necessary adjustments on his camera, then started shooting. There was only time enough to take two photographs before the monster sank out of sight.

It was in 1934 that Dr. Wilson snapped the picture that has become known as the Surgeon's Photograph. Since that time, several well-organized expeditions and many thousands of visitors have attempted to photograph the Loch Ness Monster. A few have succeeded. None of them, though, have

The famous Surgeon's Photograph. Taken by Dr. H. K. Wilson in 1934, it is still Nessie's best picture. (Copyright Associated News-papers Limited. Courtesy of the London Daily Mail)

managed to get a picture as good as the one Dr. Wilson took in 1934.

The Surgeon's Photograph appeared on the front page of the London *Daily Mail*. It showed a long neck, a snakelike head, and a huge, rather barrel-shaped body. At an estimated distance of twenty-five feet behind the body, a dark object could be seen just below the surface of the water. No one could tell what it was, but many people believed it to be the creature's tail.

Zoologists and biologists spent long hours poring over the photograph. They agreed that there was no creature like it known to science. Everything about it contradicted the laws of nature. The head was impossibly small, the neck was impossibly long, and the body was impossibly large. Besides, the creature—if it really was a creature—could not possibly live in a freshwater loch.

The majority of scientists refused to take an open stand or publish their opinion. They were quite content to say that it was an interesting photograph, but that it lacked detail and really proved nothing. One declared that it was a picture of an otter in the act of diving. Another believed it showed a seal in the act of diving. Still another solemnly expressed the belief that it was the root of a tree shot from an unusual angle.

Poor Dr. Wilson got so tired of the whole business that he absolutely refused to discuss it with anyone. Just the thought of the Loch Ness Monster was enough to make the doctor sick.

The next person to get a good close look at the monster was a teen-age girl from the little town of Fort Augustus. She had taken a summer job with the Pimley family who lived on the extreme western end of the loch.

The girl was having a cup of coffee about six o'clock one

morning when she spotted an enormous creature on one of the gravel banks. It was the biggest and strangest animal she had ever seen. With a pair of binoculars she found in the living room, she was able to see the creature perfectly.

It seemed that the animal was taking a leisurely sunbath. From time to time, it turned itself around slowly. The girl later said that it stretched and arched its back like a giant cat. She was tempted to call Mr. and Mrs. Pimley so that they could also watch the strange creature, but then decided against it. They might be angry if they were awakened so early in the morning, she thought.

The Pimleys were very angry indeed. Pimley, in fact, was terribly tempted to shoot the girl, and he told her so. He had rented a cottage facing the loch because he had hoped to see the monster. The binoculars the girl had borrowed had been bought especially for that purpose.

When he had regained his composure, Pimley asked the girl to tell him exactly what the monster had looked like.

"Oh, I really can't say," the girl replied brightly. "I've never seen anything before that looked like that thing."

It took a bit of an effort, but Pimley finally got a satisfactory description. According to the girl's account, the creature she had seen had a long giraffelike neck and a ridiculously small head. The enormous body was gray in color and the skin appeared to be like the skin of an elephant. It had two very short front legs that she thought might be flippers. She had watched the thing for about twenty-five minutes altogether. At the end of that time, the creature lowered its head, slipped quietly into the water, and disappeared.

An examination of the gravel bank revealed little. There was a small depression where the monster had apparently been basking in the sun. A branch had been pressed down

26

among the gravel stones and that was all there was to be seen.

But Pimley had now caught an acute case of monster fever. For the rest of the summer, he spent most of his time scanning the loch with his binoculars. Nessie was sighted by quite a few other people during the course of the summer, but the unlucky Pimley never did manage to see her.

Chapter 7

The monster fired everyone's imagination. The idea of a huge unidentified creature lurking in the murky depths of Loch Ness intrigued people. In some cases, of course, it appealed to their sense of the ridiculous.

A German even tried to use the monster to earn himself some easy money. He wrote a letter to a Scottish newspaper saying that he had recently spent a vacation in the Highlands. While there, he had been fortunate enough to capture the Loch Ness Monster. He had brought it back to Germany with him and it was presently tied up in a mountain lake in Bavaria where it seemed to be quite happy.

Then he told them his proposition. If the people of Scotland paid him a certain amount of money, they could have their monster back. If they refused, the monster would be sold to a German circus and would never again be seen in Scotland.

The editor of the newspaper wrote to the German and thanked him for his kind offer to sell them the monster he had captured in Loch Ness. The German, he said, was quite welcome to keep the creature. Scotland still had more monsters than it really needed, the editor explained.

It was at about this time that the search for the strange creature began in earnest. The first group arrived early in the summer of 1934. LOCH NESS MONSTER EXPEDITION FROM MONTE CARLO had been painted on their car in bold black letters. Their objective was to photograph the unidentified creature at close range. The film would then be shown in movie theaters in Europe and America and would make them all very rich.

Three days later, the Monte Carlo expedition was back in Inverness. They had an important announcement to make to the press. The announcement declared that the Loch Ness Monster was nothing more than a legend. The expedition had circled the loch several times and hadn't even seen a mini-monster.

Before leaving the Highlands, the group stopped at a garage. When they drove away, LOCH NESS MONSTER EXPEDITION FROM MONTE CARLO could no longer be seen on their car.

The next expedition was made up of two young Germans. Their plan seemed like a reasonable one. They were going to rent bicycles and pedal round and round the loch. Whenever they saw the monster, they would hop off and photograph it from different angles.

They seemed rather startled when someone pointed out to them that a bicycle trip around the loch involved seventy-two miles of pedaling. Nevertheless, they rented two light-weight English bikes and set off on their big adventure.

When they returned the following evening, they were flushed with triumph. Their expedition had been unbelievably successful. They had photographed the monster splashing playfully around only a few yards offshore. They had also managed to get pictures of the monster asleep on a sandbank and eating a goat in a pine forest.

29

An understandably cynical Highlander listened to their story and tried to hide his smile. It was a pity, he told them, that they hadn't been fortunate enough to get a picture of the monster climbing a tree or having lunch in the Drumnadrochit Hotel.

Someone else gently suggested that the Germans have their film developed in Inverness. That way, the local residents could have a good look at the monster, he told them. This the two Germans refused to do. The editor of an important magazine in Germany was going to give them a great deal of money for their film, they said, and they were anxious to get home and collect it.

Unfortunately, their departure from Inverness was delayed. The police had been informed that two young monster hunters had left the Foyers Hotel without paying for their rooms, drinks, or meals. It also developed that the two men had brought the rented bicycles onto the train with them.

The Loch Ness Monster expedition from Germany came to an unhappy end when the heavy door of the Inverness jail slammed shut behind its two members.

Chapter 8

The first really serious expedition was organized by Sir Edward Mountain in July of 1934. In recent years, expeditions have been financed by universities, scientific organizations, film companies, newspapers, and the like. Sir Edward, however, had to pay all the costs himself.

It was quite by chance that Sir Edward organized his expedition. He was an enthusiastic angler and had rented Beaufort Castle on Loch Ness for the summer. There are plenty of brown trout, sea trout, and salmon in the loch and he was looking forward to a season of good fishing.

He didn't get it. His plans were changed by the Loch Ness Monster.

Like so many others, Sir Edward became fascinated by the mystery of the loch. The Highlanders trusted him and told him their stories. It wasn't long before he was absolutely convinced that a huge creature lived somewhere in the dark depths.

But where? And what was it? And how could he get a close look at it?

These were difficult questions and Sir Edward gave them

a great deal of thought. To drain the loch was, of course, not a sensible solution. The loch's average depth was roughly seven hundred feet and it covered fourteen thousand acres. Draining the loch would give him a close look at Nessie, but it might also have a disastrous effect on the Scottish Highlands. That idea had to be rejected.

The next plan also presented serious problems. If he could somehow get close enough to the monster, reasoned Sir Edward, he *might* be able to stun her temporarily with an electric current. There was no way of knowing, though, whether the stunned monster would float on the surface or sink to the bottom.

There were two other drawbacks as well. An electric shock strong enough to stun the monster might be strong enough to kill half the fish in the loch. It might also kill the men handling the electrical equipment.

That plan, too, was discarded.

Sir Edward finally came up with a plan he thought might work. He would need a certain amount of luck, but the odds seemed to be reasonably good. The loch was twenty-four miles long. If he hired twenty reliable men and posted them a mile or two apart, they would be able to watch the entire length of the loch. It would then be most difficult for Nessie to appear on the surface and not be seen.

Hiring twenty reliable watchers was no problem. Times were hard in the summer of 1934 and men were eager to earn a little extra money.

The operation was carried out with great thoroughness. Each man was issued a pair of binoculars, a camera, and a supply of film. They kept watch from eight o'clock in the morning until six o'clock at night. Every sighting of the monster had to be carefully recorded. Details of the weather, condition of the loch, and all other details had to be included.

Each night the reports were collected and taken to Beaufort Castle. Sir Edward had drawn a large-scale map and each sighting was marked in the exact spot where it had occurred. A complete record of everything connected with the sighting was also kept on file.

For the first two weeks of the operation, the weather was warm and sunny. Everything seemed to be in favor of the men keeping their lonely vigil on the shore of the loch. Nessie was sighted twenty-one times and five photographs were taken.

Then the weather changed. Ominous black clouds hid the sun. Winds and rain lashed the loch. The watchers shivered miserably in the cold and wet.

The bad weather lasted for sixteen consecutive days and proved one thing. It proved that the monster didn't like stormy weather. Not once in all that time did she appear on the surface.

Chapter 9

The expedition lasted for a month. Although it hadn't really been a howling success, Sir Edward was now absolutely convinced that there was something very unusual in Loch Ness.

He felt that he couldn't give up the search entirely, so one of the men was kept on the job. The solitary watcher was given a movie camera with a telephoto lens. He was posted at a position on the loch where most of the sightings had taken place.

The five photographs taken during the first two weeks of the expedition were somewhat disappointing. They had been taken at long range and lacked detail. Photographing a dark object on a dark surface is a complicated business. Results are almost certain to be poor. Then, too, the monster sometimes moved at an incredible speed. At other times it was churning up a storm of spray.

Sir Edward realized how terribly difficult it would be to get a photograph of the monster at close range. A lot of time, a lot of money, and a lot of people would be needed. The cameras would have to be fitted with powerful telephoto lens. Weather conditions would have to be right or Nessie wouldn't come up from her home in the depths.

A view of Loch Ness—but what *is that shadow in the right fore-ground? A fish, a wave, or perhaps Nessie's tail as she disappears underwater?* (*United Press International*)

One other extremely important thing was needed and that thing was fantastically good luck. Without it, no one would ever manage to get a decent close-up photograph of the monster.

The expedition had also turned up another piece of interesting information. Twenty men had spent ten hours a day for one month searching for the monster. During that period of thirty days, the creature had been seen twenty-one times.

Simple arithmetic revealed something startling. One man spending one hour a day on the loch *might* see the monster one time in one year.

35

Oddly enough, the same thing holds true today. The Loch Ness Phenomena Investigation Bureau has spent every summer since 1962 at the loch. Monster watchers keep a constant vigil from first to last light. Their records show that there is an average of one sighting for every three hundred and fifty man-hours of watching. This corresponds almost exactly with Sir Edward Mountain's results.

It was early on a misty morning in September that Sir Edward's solitary watcher had a few exciting moments. There was a sudden commotion in the water and the monster suddenly surfaced about three-quarters of a mile offshore. The watcher immediately began shooting film. It was a very long shot even with a telephoto lens, but he could only hope for the best.

The best, unfortunately, wasn't very good. The morning was misty and the distance was great. Nessie had stayed on the surface a very short time and only ten feet of film had been shot. But those ten feet did show some type of creature swimming around in the loch.

Sir Edward was greatly excited. He phoned the editor of *Field* Magazine in London and told him what he had. A viewing of the film was arranged for the following week. The most prominent zoologists in Great Britain would be there. At last they were going to see a film of the elusive Loch Ness Monster.

There was an expectant hush when the camera began to whir. The zoologists leaned forward, their eyes focused intently on the screen. A dark-brown hump broke through the surface of the loch. Technicians at the Kodak Camera Company had estimated the hump to be fifteen feet long. There was no sign of either the head or the neck. After remaining in one position for a few seconds, the creature moved rapidly through the water. A very well-defined wake marked its path.

The monster traveled about twenty-five yards, then sank straight down into the depths.

The film ended and the lights were switched on. The zoologists looked at one another rather blankly. Finally one spoke up. "The so-called Loch Ness Monster is almost certainly a large gray seal," he announced.

To Sir Edward Mountain's utter amazement, most of the other scientists agreed. Not one of them was prepared to say that the monster *might* be some huge unidentified creature. They were all afraid to upset their zoological applecart. What they had seen could not be explained in terms of the known and they refused to associate themselves with the unknown.

Sir Edward was too disappointed to argue with these learned men. He knew perfectly well, however, that the seal theory was absurd.

Seals are friendly and curious creatures; Nessie was extremely shy. A seal was seldom more than six feet long; the monster was twenty-five feet long at the very least and probably much more. Seals never swam with the back out of the water and never sank straight down. Neither did they leave a wake. They were air-breathing mammals who spent more time out of the water than under. Seals frequently spent many hours basking in the sun, yet no one had ever seen a seal in Loch Ness.

"The zoologists in London must think the Highlanders are a bunch of half-wits who don't know a seal when they see one," Sir Edward declared bitterly. Then he added, "I don't know what the Loch Ness Monster is, but I definitely do know that it's not a seal."

Chapter 10

The years went by, but Nessie was seldom in the news. High-landers who saw her simply didn't bother to make a report. It annoyed them to know that the outside world looked upon their monster as either a seal or a huge joke. So little was heard about Nessie, in fact, that some people thought she had died.

In 1939, Great Britain declared war on Germany. The Loch Ness Monster was almost forgotten. The whole world was now watching a monster named Adolf Hitler.

Troops were rushed to the Scottish Highlands and some of them set up camp on the shores of Loch Ness. The soldiers knew that this was the home of the famous monster. When they weren't watching for enemy bombers, they kept an eye out for Nessie.

There were several sightings and one of them was of par-ticular interest. A member of the Royal Observer Corps was on watch when the monster came to the surface just two hundred and fifty yards from him. It was early in the morning and conditions were ideal. The observer had a perfect oppor-tunity to study the creature through his powerful binoculars. He saw an amazing sight.

A body thirty feet long could be seen clearly. A graceful neck was raised five feet above the water. Something resembling an odd-shaped fin or crest ran down the back of the neck. The eyes were large and prominent.

The observer believed that the creature was feeding. It would lower its head and neck in the same manner as a swan until both were completely submerged. When the head and neck were brought out of the water, the creature would shake them vigorously.

Finally, the monster disappeared. It didn't dive. It simply sank down so gently that there was scarcely a ripple.

Germany surrendered in 1945 and the world slowly returned to its normal state of rather disordered order. Adolf Hitler, the monster in Germany, was dead. Nessie, the monster in Loch Ness, was very much alive and going stronger than ever. She was still the world's most famous unsolved mystery.

Chapter 11

During the summer of 1951, Nessie again made the headlines and had her picture on the front page of a large daily newspaper. The photograph was taken by a woodsman named Lachlan Stewart.

Stewart lived in a cottage about a hundred feet from the water's edge. His family and Taylor Hay, another woodsman, shared the cottage with him.

Men in the Forestry Commission began work at eight o'clock. Stewart, however, had a cow to milk and always got up at six. On this particular morning, he happened to glance out of the window while drinking a cup of coffee. Something he at first thought was a fast motorboat was speeding down the center of the loch.

This seemed strange to him. People seldom ventured out onto the loch at such an early hour. But that wasn't all. Speeding motorboats usually made a fearful racket and the morning was perfectly still.

And then Stewart realized what he was seeing! After alerting his wife and telling Taylor Hay to hurry, he grabbed his cheap box camera and ran down to the water. His wife and Mr. Hay soon joined him.

40

The creature was now much closer and they had an excellent view. The head appeared to be the same size and shape as the head of a sheep. None of them saw ears or horns. Neither did they notice eyes.

Three large humps rose about three feet out of the water. The head and neck were not raised, but were sticking straight out. They seemed to be the same distance above the surface as the humps. Every few seconds, the head was lowered into the water, then promptly raised once more to the original position.

The three people watched in grim fascination as the monster came closer and closer. It was no more than forty yards away when Lachlan Stewart raised his cheap little box camera. The viewfinder clearly showed the three humps. Stewart held his breath and quickly clicked the shutter.

He had advanced the film and was preparing to photograph the head and neck when the monster veered suddenly and came straight at them. The three people turned and ran and no one could blame them for that.

But Nessie had played her little game. Instead of coming ashore, she turned around in a shower of spray and raced off toward the center of the loch. Three hundred yards from the water's edge, she came to a halt and sank slowly out of sight.

Scientists and newspapermen beat a path to Stewart's door. A reporter from the *Daily Express* developed the film and got an excellent picture of three angular humps, each separated by several feet of water.

Stewart couldn't imagine what all the fuss was about, but he cooperated fully with his interviewers. His absolute sincerity left no room for doubt. He had seen exactly what he described and he described it well.

Everything about his experience was amazing. His estimate of the total length of the creature, however, was the

The Lachlan Stewart photo taken in the summer of 1951. (*The London* Daily Express)

most amazing thing of all. Both Stewart and Hay believed that the head and neck measured about six feet in length. Each of the three humps was roughly five feet long. They were separated by approximately eight feet of water. What Stewart thought must have been the end of the creature's tail was causing a slight commotion about twenty feet behind the last hump.

The interviewer did some quick mental arithmetic. If Stewart's figures were correct, the monster was fifty-seven feet long.

This made Nessie a truly monstrous monster.

Chapter **12**

After many years of scoffing at the idea of a monster in Loch Ness, the scientists finally began to scratch their beards and give the matter some serious thought. Perhaps there really is some strange creature there, they whispered to one another. After all, these stories have been going on for years.

This wasn't quite true. Stories about the monster in Loch Ness had been circulating for centuries! The first written report, in fact, dates back to the sixth century. It occurs in Saint Adamnan's biography of Saint Columba.

The report was translated from the Latin by Father J. A. Carruth, a monk at Saint Benedict's Abbey. The abbey is located at the western end of the loch. Father Carruth had always been extremely interested in the Loch Ness Monster and had seen it several times.

The chapter referring to the creature in the loch is entitled, "Of the Driving Away of a Certain Water Monster by Virtue of Prayer of the Holy Man."

Father Carruth's translation follows:

When the blessed man was staying for some days in the province of the Picts, he found it necessary to

43

cross the water Ness; and when he came to the bank thereof, he sees some of the inhabitants burying a poor unfortunate man, whom, as those who were burying him themselves reported, some water Monster had, a little before, snatched at as he was swimming and bitten with a most savage bite, and whose hapless corpse some men who came in a boat to give assistance, though too late, caught hold of it by putting out hooks.

The blessed man, however, on hearing this, directs that some of his companions shall swim out and bring to him the boat that is on the other side, sailing it across. On hearing this direction of the holy and famous man, Lugne Mocumin, obeying without delay, throws off all his clothes except his undergarment, and casts himself into the water. Now the Monster, which was not so much satiated as made eager for prey, was lying hid in the bottom of the river, but perceiving that the water above was disturbed by him who was crossing, suddenly emerged, and swimming to the man as he was crossing, rushed up at him with a great roar and open mouth.

Then the blessed man looked on, while all who were there, the heathen as well as the brethren, were stricken with terrible great terror; and with his holy hand raised on high he did form the sign of the cross in the empty air, invoked the name of God, and commanded the fierce Monster, crying, "Think not to go further nor touch thou that man. Quick! Go back!" Then the beast on hearing this voice of the saint, was terrified and fled backwards more rapidly than he had come, as if dragged by cords,

44

although it had come so close to Lugne as he swam, that there was not more than the length of a punt pole between the man and the Monster.

This is indeed a strange tale. There are literally hundreds of lochs in the Scottish Highlands. It is surely more than a coincidence that Saint Columba happened to bump into a monster at Loch Ness.

Parts of the report are impossible to explain. Saint Adamnan says that the monster "rushed up . . . with a great roar." Since that time, no one has heard as much as a squeak out of Nessie. But the report also says that everyone was "stricken with terrible great terror." It is possible, then, that people stricken with terrible great terror might honestly have believed that they *had* heard the monster roar.

Neither is it possible to explain the death of the poor unfortunate man who was "bitten with a most savage bite." Nessie just isn't the kind of monster who goes around biting people. It is true that she's nearly frightened some people to death, but this wasn't really her fault.

There seems to be only one possible explanation and it may not be a very good one. If there are both nice people and naughty people, then there can also be nice monsters and naughty monsters. Nessie is a nice, well-behaved monster who never causes trouble. Her ancestor, however, must have been a very naughty monster or she wouldn't have given the poor unfortunate man a most savage bite.

Nearly a thousand years after Saint Columba's experience with the monster, another one of Nessie's ancestors made a bad name for herself. This particular incident is recorded in *A History of Scotland* and took place at Loch Ness in 1527.

This terrible beast issuing out of the water early one morning about mid summer, he did very easily and without any force or straining of himself over-throw huge oaks with his tail and therewith killed outright three men that hunted him with three strokes of his tail, the rest of them saving themselves in trees thereabouts, whilst the aforesaid monster returned to the loch.

This account, of course, is exaggerated, but the ring of truth is still there. Once again, the scene of the action is Loch Ness.

The report refers to the creature as a terrible beast. In the last few years, people who have seen Nessie at close range have called her loathsome, hideous, an abomination, and a horrible beast.

It's also of interest to note that Nessie's habits seem to be pretty much the same as her ancestors'. She, too, is more apt to make an appearance very early on a summer morning. She also has been seen on land on a number of occasions. Although people have described Nessie's tail as being very powerful, no one has yet seen her use it to kill men or overthrow huge oaks. This is most likely the sort of thing Nessie wouldn't even consider doing. At all times, she has conducted herself like a lady.

One of the ancient descriptions of the monster is far more colorful than it is accurate. In this case, the creature is referred to as a worm. "The dreadful beast, the direful wurrum—half fish and half dragon—that still survives in a mountain loch."

Nessie has been called many things in her time, but it hardly seems fair to call her a direful wurrum.

Chapter **13**

Once the scientists had decided to take the Loch Ness Monster seriously, they found themselves faced with some tough questions. The answers were never easy to find. Many of the questions, in fact, are still unanswered.

The first question was: How in the world did the monster get into Loch Ness in the first place? The answer to that should have been simple, but it wasn't at all.

The monster's original home had been the sea. There could be no doubt whatsoever about that. So what was she doing in a freshwater loch? Had she somehow found her way in from the North Sea or the Atlantic Ocean?

A little research showed that this was unlikely. Loch Ness is a part of the Caledonian Canal. The canal was built in 1823. It cuts across northern Scotland from southwest to northeast. Salmon can easily make it through the canal, but a monster would have an awfully tough time of it. It would have to pass through a total of nineteen locks on the trip. To do this without being seen simply wasn't possible. It couldn't even be done at night because the locks are never opened after dark.

It wasn't likely, either, that the creature had come in by

way of the river Ness. Although the river is wide enough, it is only a few feet deep. A monster splashing along for mile after mile through shallow water would be most unhappy.

Besides, the Ness River flows right through the middle of the town of Inverness. It's true that some strange things have been seen in Inverness, but nobody has yet seen an honest-to-goodness monster in the downtown area.

It was probably safe to assume then that the creature had not entered by way of the canal or the river Ness. Neither was it reasonable to think that it had casually strolled overland from the sea to the loch. There was one more possibility that had to be explored.

Many Highlanders believed that Loch Ness was connected to the sea by underwater passages. In many ways, this theory made sense. It meant that the monster could come and go as it pleased. This, of course, would explain the long absences from home. If considerable time elapsed between sightings, it was because Nessie had decided to go off to sea for a while.

A little investigation punched some rather large holes in this theory. The surface of Loch Ness is fifty-two feet above mean sea level. If there were a subterranean passage, the water would flow out of the loch until the mouth of the passage was exposed.

The tunnel theory, however, can't be thrown out entirely. Eight fair-sized rivers and quite a number of small streams flow into Loch Ness. If as much water flowed in as flowed out, then there *could* be an underwater passage, but it would have to be a small one. Whether or not Nessie would want to battle a stiff current through miles of inky-black tunnel is something only Nessie knows.

One thing, at any rate, was clear. If the monster could not have gotten into the loch from the sea, then it had been in the loch all the time. But how could that be? "All the time" would mean that it had been there forever. A saltwater creature could not possibly have been in a freshwater loch all the time.

This was one puzzle the geologists were able to solve. Up until five or ten thousand years ago, they explained, there had been no such thing as Loch Ness. The loch was glacial in origin and had once been a part of the sea. It had not become a loch until toward the end of the Ice Age.

During the Ice Age, an enormous sheet of ice came grinding and crunching its way south through the Northern Hemisphere. Nobody really knows why. Some think that the weight of the polar ice caps was so off-balance that the crust of the earth slipped on its core. Others think that something went wrong with the amount of heat being put out by the sun. Or a cloud of some type of celestial dust got between the earth and the sun. Without the heat of the sun, the climate changed drastically. It kept getting colder and colder.

Geologists believe that the sheet of ice crushing Scotland was more than three thousand feet thick. As it crunched south, it knocked the tops off mountains and gouged out deep valleys. The weight of the ice cap was so tremendous that it literally pushed poor little Scotland farther down into the crust of the earth.

After a few thousand years of this, the climate changed. The sun broke the clouds. The weather became warmer and the ice began to melt. Without its crushing burden of ice, the land slowly began to rise. It rose until Loch Ness was no longer an arm of the sea. It was now a lake filled with nice fresh water.

And somewhere in that nice fresh water was a huge saltwater creature. A few thousand years later, this creature would be known to all the world as the Loch Ness Monster.

Chapter **14**

There were still some cynics. A saltwater creature could not live in a freshwater loch, they said.

The cynics were soon proved to be wrong. It was pointed out to them that other sea creatures were living quite happily in bodies of fresh water. They had been cut off from the sea by geologic upheavals, but they were still alive and doing fine.

The sharks in Central America's Lake Nicaragua was given as one example. Another one was the freshwater seals in Canada and Russia. Freshwater dolphins play happily in Chinese, Indian, and Brazilian lakes.

The conclusion is obvious. If dolphins, seals, and sharks can readily adapt themselves to freshwater conditions, then monsters should also be able to do it.

With that out of the way, another question immediately came popping up. Nessie had been cut off from her home in the sea during the final stages of the Ice Age. This means that she had already celebrated at least five thousand birthdays.

For once, the zoologists were in complete agreement. They all agreed that it would be absolutely impossible for any living creature, even an unidentified monster, to reach the ripe old age of five thousand years. These things just didn't happen.

But how could this incredible thing be explained? The monster was a sea creature that had almost certainly been trapped in Loch Ness thousands of years ago. It couldn't have lived all those years, yet the creature had been seen by dozens and dozens of perfectly reliable witnesses.

There was only one logical explanation. Nessie was not the monster who had been cut off from the sea all those years back. She was merely a direct descendant of the original monsters.

Parts of the puzzle now fell easily into place. The passing of the Ice Age had left a man monster and a lady monster trapped in Loch Ness. They had raised a family and that family had raised another family. This had gone on for countless generations and Nessie was a member of the present generation.

Although it may seem strange to think of Nessie as a wife and mother, it's probably safe to assume that she is. Several eyewitnesses have reported seeing two separate monsters, one considerably larger than the other. As far as is known, baby monsters have been reported on only one occasion. They were seen by two boys who attended the abbey school.

The boys were questioned separately by Dom Cyril Dieckhoff, a monk at Saint Benedict's Abbey. The monk was convinced that the boys were telling the truth. Although they hadn't known that they were going to be questioned, their stories were identical in every respect. It hadn't occurred to either one of them that the creatures they had seen might in some manner be connected with the Loch Ness Monster.

The loch was very calm on the bright and sunny day the boys spotted the creatures. They were drifting along lazily when the boy in the stern spotted three strange shapes swimming along behind the boat. Each one was about three feet in length. "Hey, Tony," he called to his friend Anthony Considine, "come over here and look at these things."

Considine at first thought they were eels, but he quickly discarded that idea. The creatures he was watching had a pair of limbs in front and another pair in back. The front limbs were small and shaped like flippers. As far as Considine could determine, the front flippers didn't seem to be doing anything except waving around in the water. The larger limbs in the back were doing all the work. They were held close to the body and propelled it through the water with a kicking action.

"They're not eels," declared Considine. "Eels don't have limbs and their necks are different."

"They might be big lizards," suggested his companion.

Considine didn't think so. He didn't know whether or not there were lizards in Scotland, but he was pretty sure that a lizard couldn't swim underwater for so long.

The three creatures soon disappeared from sight and the boys promptly lost interest. When they mentioned the strange incident to their parents, it was almost as an afterthought.

Their parents and Dom Cyril Dieckhoff, however, had a pretty good idea of what the boys had seen. They believed that Nessie was raising a family. The three mini-monsters were her children.

Chapter 15

If there have been monsters in Loch Ness for five thousand years, inquire the cynics, then why have no dead bodies been washed ashore?

This is another question for which there is no handy cut-and-dried answer. Highlanders, however, say that the loch never gives up its dead.

This is true in one well-known case and may be true in others. A farmer decided that he could get rich in a hurry if he managed to capture the Loch Ness Monster. The poor fellow must either have been very short of money or very soft in the head.

At any rate, he built himself a flat-bottomed boat. A winch with a hand crank was installed in the rear and several hundred yards of strong rope were wound onto it. One of the local blacksmiths fashioned an enormous hook for him. The bait was the carcass of a sheep.

Day after day, the man rowed slowly around the loch with the baited hook in the water while his neighbors hooted with laughter. The days melted into weeks, but the monster refused to take the bait. Perhaps it only feeds at night, the monster hunter told himself, and thereafter he didn't start fishing until the late afternoon.

One morning his empty boat was found floating near Urquhart Castle. The hook was still baited. Everything else was in good order, but the man was never seen again. Nobody knows what happened to him.

Loch Ness is dark and deep. There are many places where a person can step off the bank straight into several hundred feet of water. Although there is no tide to wash a body ashore, there are strong underwater currents that might keep a body from ever rising to the surface.

There are other reasons as well. Scientists still do not know whether Nessie is a vertebrate or an invertebrate monster. They can't tell, therefore, whether her dead ancestors were even capable of floating. They may have dropped dead and sunk like a stone.

Quite a few people believe that Nessie lives in a large cavern deep down in the loch. Nobody knows for sure that such caverns or caves actually exist. So much about the loch is still a mystery. But if these underwater rooms do exist, they would probably not be affected by the currents. A monster who died at home would remain there until it had decomposed completely. Unless, of course, it was eaten by the other monsters.

That brings up another question. What does Nessie eat? Fortunately, this was one of the few questions about the monster that could be answered without too much difficulty.

First, though, the scientists had to discover whether Nessie was a meat-eating or plant-eating animal.

This was a simple matter. A survey by the scientists showed that the loch supported only a very meager plant life. There was simply not enough vegetation available to keep a monster strong, healthy, and happy.

The ruins of Urquhart Castle at Inverness lend an appropriately eerie note to Loch Ness. (Wide World Photos)

Although there is a shortage of plant life, there are plenty of fish for Nessie to feast on. The eels in Loch Ness are thick and juicy and there are tremendous numbers of them. Pike, a fish hated by Scottish fishermen, often weigh fifty pounds or more, and the anglers heartily hope that Nessie will eat all of them. Fifteen-pound trout and thirty-pound salmon have been caught in the loch and there are other smaller types of fish.

On several occasions, people have actually watched Nessie fishing for her dinner. A group of eight people were standing on Temple Pier one afternoon when salmon started leaping all over the place. It was apparent that something had frightened the fish. Then the watchers saw a dark form slicing through the water at great speed. A brownish hump rose above the surface of the loch, leaving a marked wake behind it. The salmon could hardly be blamed for wanting to get out of there as quickly as possible. Nessie has a huge appetite and

55

there's nothing better than a few fresh salmon for lunch.

Every fisherman knows that the best time to catch fish is in the early morning and in the evening. Nessie knows this, too. She even seems to know the spots in the loch where she's most apt to catch fish.

The Ness is one of the best salmon rivers in Scotland. Although it is only six miles long, it is the loch's natural outlet to the sea. Many thousands of salmon pass through the river Ness and Loch Ness on their way to the spawning grounds. Not all of them get there.

As mentioned earlier, the river Ness flows through the center of the pretty little town of Inverness. A great number of men in the town have an almost incurable disease called salmon fever. This sickness becomes much more prevalent during the spring and fall salmon migrations. Catching a salmon is the only cure for this dread disease.

When there is a particularly good run of salmon in the river, business in Inverness nearly grinds to a stop. Those who aren't fishing are lined up on the banks and bridges watching the fun.

Children on the way to school might see their teacher casting a fly. Doctors are apt to see their most seriously ill patients struggling with a large salmon. Employers can be seen pleading with their employees to please come to work.

Salmon that make it through the river Ness without getting caught have to face a new danger. The name of this new danger is Nessie. She knows that there are a lot of nice fish heading her way and she's ready to give them a warm welcome.

Fish entering the loch from the river have to swim past a spot called Tor Point. It's probably more than a coincidence that the Loch Ness Monster has been frequently sighted in that area.

Chapter **16**

Efforts to classify the Loch Ness Monster had the scientists crawling the walls and tearing their beards. The descriptions they heard from eyewitnesses merely confused them. There ain't no such animal, they told one another.

There was so much about Nessie that the zoologists still had to learn. The only actual information they had was that an enormous unidentified creature of some type lived in the loch. They still hadn't been able to learn whether it was a vertebrate or an invertebrate creature. Neither did they know whether it was a mammal or a reptile or a fish—or what have you?

Perhaps, thought the zoologists and marine biologists, the sea will give us a clue. After all, Nessie's ancestors had originally come from the sea. If they could find and identify one of her relatives, their problem would be solved.

It wasn't long before the scientists found themselves wallowing helplessly about in unknown waters. The things they did find confused them so badly that they didn't know what to think. Instead of solving their problem, they found that Nessie's identity had become even more complicated.

57

For a time, the scientists thought they were on the right track. Over the years, many seafaring men had reported seeing a great sea serpent. The sightings had been recorded in ships' logs and discussed in ports around the world. A British naval commander called R.T. Gould had even written a book on great sea serpents. He had talked to sailors who had seen them and he had faithfully recorded their descriptions.

Zoologists and marine biologists who studied Commander Gould's book made a startling discovery. Descriptions of the great sea serpent and descriptions of the Loch Ness Monster were strikingly similar in many ways.

Some witnesses reported seeing great sea serpents no more than thirty feet in length. Others had seen giants measuring over a hundred feet long. This shouldn't surprise anyone. After all, a baby python is only a fraction as large as Papa Python. There's no reason in the world why all great sea serpents and all monsters have to be the same size.

Descriptions of the head also tallied closely. People had described Nessie's head as snakelike, sheeplike, and horselike. The same words were used in reports of the great sea serpent. The smaller the monster, the smaller the head. Everyone agreed, too, that the head appeared to be disproportionately small in relation to the great length of body.

The neck was always described as very long and sinuous. It was slender, but broadened considerably when it joined the body. When the neck of the great sea serpent was in an upright position, it reached as much as eighteen to twenty feet above the water. Nessie, it seems, has no more than five or six feet of neck to stick out.

It's interesting to note here the probable size of the monsters. One scientist states that a creature able to raise its head six feet above the water would probably be about eighty feet long. A creature able to raise its head twenty feet above the

Do these "monsters" from past centuries, drawn from reports by reliable eyewitnesses, bear any resemblance to Nessie?

The Valhalla's Sea Monster based on a rough sketch made by an "eyewitness." (Brown Brothers)

The great sea serpent, according to Bishop Pontoppidan. (New York Public Library)

A sea serpent from the Travel Book of Olaus Magnus, *1555. (The Bettman Archive)*

water might be two hundred or even three hundred feet in length. A monster as long as a football field ought to be large enough to keep anyone happy.

No one has yet claimed to have seen an eighty-foot monster in Loch Ness. That doesn't mean, though, that there aren't any. There is at least one scientist who is convinced that there are. It's possible, too, that the loch is hiding an even larger one. During the summer of 1969, Professor D.G. Tucker of Birmingham University tracked an "obviously animate object" in Loch Ness with electronic sonar equipment. The obviously animate object was a giant of well over a hundred feet in length. Professor Tucker, however, is a cautious man. He is careful not to say that the creature was Nessie. What he does say is, "It's a temptation to suppose that the echoes came from the fabulous Loch Ness Monster."

The great sea serpent had a few other things in common with the Loch Ness Monster. It, too, had a large and supple body. Sailors' reports declared that the sea serpent had a number of humps and that the humps were separated by several feet of water. Lachlan Stewart, Taylor Hay, and many others had described Nessie in exactly the same way.

There was agreement, too, on the comparative speeds of the two creatures. Many observers had declared that they were incredibly fast. Witnesses have estimated Nessie's speed at thirty miles an hour. There's no way of knowing, of course, whether or not she was going wide open at the time. She might be able to travel even faster when she really has to.

In spite of their great speed and great size, the creatures move through the water as gracefully as a swan. It's not possible to see what makes them go, but they go like a streak. The boys who watched the baby monsters in Loch Ness stated that they had two pairs of flippers. The back ones were held close to the body and propelled it with a kicking action. It's probably safe to assume then that both Nessie and her saltwater cousins propel themselves in the same way. There's also the possibility that they use their tails to help them on their journeys.

Now that the zoologists and marine biologists had finished their homework and compared notes, it was time to ask the big question. Was the Loch Ness Monster a great sea serpent?

After stroking their beards thoughtfully, they came up with the answer. No, they said. No, the Loch Ness Monster is very definitely not a great sea serpent.

Why not?

That question was a very easy one to answer. There was

61

no scientific proof that such a creature as a great sea serpent even existed. If there was no scientific proof of its existence, then it couldn't possibly exist. The men who claimed they had seen it were a bunch of half-witted sailors with too much rum in their bellies and too much saltwater in their eyes.

Once again the men of science declared that there ain't no such animal.

Chapter **17**

Over a hundred years ago, a British sailing ship was returning home from a voyage to the East Indies. The captain, three officers, and three crew members were standing on the quarterdeck enjoying the warm summer evening. The nearest land was hundreds of miles behind them. Suddenly, one of the officers rushed to the rail and pointed at something in the water. It was an enormous serpent.

The seven men watched in astonishment as the creature rapidly approached the ship. Although the men had spent many long years at sea, they had never seen anything like it. What was a snake doing so far from home? they wondered. Then they realized that it was a great sea serpent that they were seeing.

The monster seemed to be in a great hurry. It didn't deviate in the slightest degree from its course. Neither did it look anywhere but straight ahead. The silent sailing ship interested it not at all. Although the serpent was moving along at a good clip, the men on board were unable to tell how it propelled itself through the water.

In his report to the Admiralty, the captain stated that the

creature was at the very least sixty feet long. It was dark brown in color. The throat was yellowish-white and it had a mane somewhat like the mane of a horse.

Someone in the Admiralty apparently didn't believe the captain's story. He wanted to know how many rums the captain had drunk before sighting the sea serpent.

Captain R. J. Cringle, master of the *Umfuli,* had a good close look at a strange creature off the east coast of Africa. He wrote:

> It was rushing through the water at a great speed, and was throwing water from its breast as a vessel throws water from her bows. I saw full fifteen feet of its head and neck on several occasions. The body was all the time visible. The base, or body, from which the neck sprang was much thicker than the neck itself, and I should not, therefore, call it a serpent. Had it been breezy enough to ruffle the water, or hazy, I should have had some doubt about the creature; but the sea being perfectly smooth I had not the slightest doubt in my mind as to its being a sea monster.

Poor Captain Cringle! Like so many others who had reported seeing a monster, he was cruelly ridiculed by scoffers and cynics. He even refused an interview with Commander Gould who was then writing his book on great sea serpents.

"I have been ridiculed so much on this that I must decline to have anything more to do with it," he told Gould. "I am certainly convinced that what I saw was a living creature, but I have been so ridiculed about the thing that I wish it had been someone else who saw the sea monster rather than me."

Another sea monster or great sea serpent was sighted the

same year in which the unlucky Captain Cringle saw his. Oddly enough, this spectacular sighting took place off the coast of Scotland, not more than an hour's drive from Loch Ness.

Dr. Farquhar Matheson and his wife were sailing merrily along in a small boat on the narrow strait that lies between the mainland and the Isle of Skye. It was a beautiful, clear day. The sun was warm and there was scarcely a cloud to be seen. The doctor's hand was resting lightly on the tiller, but suddenly he took a good firm grip. A strange creature of some type was rising out of the water. His wife also saw it and she went pale with fear.

The doctor was too fascinated to be frightened. The beast kept rising and rising until its head appeared to be as high above the water as the mast of the little boat. Less than two hundred yards separated the boat from the beast. It was really too close for comfort. The doctor's wife begged him to turn around, but the doctor's intellectual curiosity was greater than his sense of caution.

Dr. Matheson wrote later:

I saw clearly that it was a large sea monster, probably of the saurian type. It was brown in color, shining, and with a sort of ruffle at the junction of the head and neck. I can think of nothing to which to compare it so well as the head and neck of a giraffe, only the neck was much longer, and the head was not set upon the neck like that of a giraffe; that is, it was not so much at right angles to it as a continuation of it in the same line. I saw no body, only a ripple of water where the body should be. I should judge, however, that there must have been a large base of body to support such a neck. It was

65

not a sea serpent, but a much larger and substantial beast—something in the nature of a gigantic lizard, I should think.

In 1953, many scientists were still insisting that the great sea serpent was a myth and that the Loch Ness Monster was a joke. Although they knew that hundreds of reliable witnesses had reported seeing the great sea serpent and hundreds more claimed to have seen Nessie, they refused to believe the reports. It was the same old story. There was no scientific proof that these creatures existed—therefore, they didn't exist.

Then something occurred that had the zoologists and marine biologists doing backflips!

Dr. J. L. Smith, a zoology professor at Rhodes University in South Africa, was called to examine a fish someone had caught in the Indian Ocean. The fish was a funny-looking thing about five feet long. Soft hollow spines ran up and down the length of its ugly, scaly body. Everything about the creature was repulsive.

The professor took one look at the creature and his eyes almost popped out of his head. And it's no wonder! The fish he was looking at could not possibly exist. Why not? Well, because it had been extinct for forty or fifty million years. That's why. Dr. Smith even had fossils to prove it.

The ugly fish was a coelacanth and belonged to the Triassic Age. The last of the coelacanths had died many millions of years ago. It was almost impossible for the professor to believe his eyes. If a dinosaur had walked into his living room he could not have been more surprised.

Now here was a pretty kettle of fish. The coelacanth had broken every rule in the book. Apparently it just didn't know that when something became extinct, it stayed extinct. It just didn't simply pop up again fifty million years later. Things like that didn't happen. A fossil was supposed to stay a fossil. It was not supposed to break a scientific law by coming back to life. This wasn't the thing to do, because it confused the men of science.

The coelacanth, of course, had not been extinct at all. It had been swimming cheerfully around in the Mozambique Channel—and perhaps in other places—all the time. It was just that nobody had ever seen one.

But people *have* seen the great sea serpent and they *have* seen the Loch Ness Monster.

This is precisely what confuses the issue. Although the monsters have been seen, they were really not supposed to exist. The coelacanth was not supposed to exist because the last one disappeared countless ages ago. Then the ungrateful thing suddenly popped up and embarrassed everyone.

So now the scientific world had nonexistent monsters splashing around, *plus* a perfectly healthy fish that had been extinct for fifty million years.

Chapter 18

There can be no doubt but that the appearance of the coela-canth increased interest in the Loch Ness Monster. A few dramatic sightings also put Nessie back on the front page of the newspapers. In at least two instances, the monster gave people a terrible fright.

Mrs. Greta Finlay, a native of Inverness, had brought her small son to the loch for a fishing holiday. Her house trailer was parked near the shore at Tor Point. She was preparing lunch one day when she heard a great splashing in the water. The commotion continued, so she and her son went to see what was going on. There, not twenty yards away, was the creature she had heard so much about, but never expected to see. "It was so close," she later told reporters, "that I could have hit it with a pebble."

It was a terrifying sight and Mrs. Finlay admits that she was paralyzed with fear. Pulling her son close to her side, they stood staring at the repulsive beast. Very few people had ever managed to get a closer or better look. Mrs. Finlay, in fact, was much closer than she wanted to be.

The witnesses were able to see about fifteen feet of the monster. The long neck was held erectly and the ridiculously small head was the same width as the neck. Two stalklike projections, each about six inches long, could be seen on top of the head. The projections ended with what were described as little blobs. Mrs. Finlay stated that the stalklike projections resembled tiny antennae or the "horns" on a snail. The skin was dark in color and appeared to be very tough.

Seeing the monster at such close range unnerved Mrs. Finlay completely. "I never want to see the thing again," she later declared. "I wouldn't even go to look if it were exhibited behind six-inch steel bars. It was a horrible creature."

Her son shared her reaction. Like most boys in the highlands of Scotland, he had loved to go fishing. But the sight of the monster changed all that for him. He refused to go near the loch again. The new fishing rod he had been given for his birthday was put away in the attic and never used.

Not satisfied with having ruined the Finlay boy's fishing, the monster next ruined a picnic.

Mr. and Mrs. G. C. Forbes of Inverness had taken two elderly English guests down to the shore of the loch for a picnic lunch. The ladies from England had, of course, heard many tales about the famous Loch Ness Monster. They assured their hosts that they just couldn't tell their friends at home that they had been to Loch Ness and not seen the monster.

Mr. Forbes smiled. He often visited the loch, but he had never seen Nessie. Neither had he ever met anyone who had seen her. Being a bank manager, Mr. Forbes had to be practical and hardheaded. Seeing was believing and he had never seen the monster.

While they were enjoying the warm afternoon sun, one of the women pointed out a disturbance in the loch. Something had obviously frightened the fish. Salmon and trout were leaping around like wild.

Then they heard an enormous splash. The people scrambled to their feet. A large dark body was slicing swiftly through the water. Five or six odd-shaped humps were clearly visible, but they couldn't see the head.

Some tourist buses were traveling down the road on the opposite side of the loch. Mr. Forbes believed that the visible part of the monster was at least as long as the buses. It was his opinion that the monster was traveling even faster than the vehicles. He estimated the creature's speed to be somewhere between forty and fifty miles an hour. The spray sparkled in the sunlight. The waves caused by the beast's passage through the water were larger than those of a fast and powerful motorboat.

Without a word to anyone, Nessie turned abruptly and raced in the direction of the Forbes's party. The potato salad, beans, and cold meat were forgotten. Everyone raced for the safety of higher ground, the two old ladies from England well in the lead. When they reached the road, they found that another party of people from Inverness were also witnessing the unusual spectacle.

The next morning, Mr. Forbes gave reporters a detailed account of his experience. A total of eight people had seen exactly what he had seen. With that many witnesses, it seemed unlikely to him that anyone would question the truth of his report.

But he was wrong. A few days later, the following letter appeared in a daily newspaper:

Dear Sir,
    Although not acquainted with Mr. G. C. Forbes, Manager of the National Bank, Inverness, I should

70

like to confirm his statement. From my viewpoint in the loch I could see Mr. Forbes distinctly on the shore with his friends and I actually saw them leap to safety when I came racing up the loch.

Might I please ask sightseers to return their empty whisky bottles, for the amount of broken glass in and around the loch is very dangerous to us amphibians.

Yours faithfully,
The Loch Ness Monster

Although this letter was written in good fun, it points out clearly why some people are reluctant to tell others that they've seen Nessie.

Even a member of the other party from Inverness declined to issue a supporting statement saying that he had been watching Nessie at the same time as Mr. Forbes and his party. "I don't wish to become known as one of those crackpots who has seen the Loch Ness Monster," he declared tersely.

Chapter 19

In spite of the fear of ridicule, reports of sightings kept coming in regularly. No one, of course, can know how many sightings were *not* reported.

On one occasion, a Highlands bus was chugging alongside the loch when one of the passengers noticed something unusual. If the girl had been a tourist, she would probably have let out a shriek. Christine Fraser, however, was not a tourist. She had lived on the loch most of her life. She had never seen the monster and wasn't even convinced that there was one. Still, there was something out there now and she called the driver's attention to it.

The driver looked—then slammed on the brakes. "It's the monster!" he cried, jumping out of the bus. His twenty-seven passengers came jumping out after him.

For the next ten minutes, twenty-eight people watched Nessie romping about the loch. These people were not tourists. They were people who lived in the Scottish Highlands. Nessie was a part of their folklore, but most of the passengers had never seen her.

But they were seeing her now, all right. Although she

was throwing up spray and creating a tremendous wake, they all had a good look at her. There were three humps in sight, the middle hump being much larger than the others. The overall length appeared to be approximately twenty-five feet. The passengers thought that Nessie might be chasing fish. She kept her head and neck completely underwater as she raced back and forth at a fearful rate.

The cynics and scoffers didn't know what to think. Twenty-eight people said that they had seen the Loch Ness Monster. Did that mean, then, that there really was such a creature? Or had they been victims of a mass hallucination? Or had it perhaps been an optical illusion? Or had every single one of the twenty-eight people on that bus been a crackpot? The cynics and scoffers didn't know.

Another impressive sighting followed soon afterward. A workman on the Glendoe Estate was approaching the loch when an amazing beast rose slowly up from the depths. It looked as though the creature was going to continue to rise forever. The creature was so close to the shore that the laborer was looking almost directly down on it.

There were twelve distinct humps, each one rising about a foot above the water. Something resembling the mane of a horse started at the back of the head and extended about four feet down the back of the neck. From time to time, the beast shook its head vigorously. The day was so clear and the man was so close that he could see individual drops of water being tossed off the mane.

For once, Nessie didn't seem to be in a hurry. She moved lazily off toward Glendoe Pier where a stream entered the loch. The man watching thought that from the rear she looked like a giant duck. He was unable to see feet, flippers, or tail and couldn't imagine what made the thing go.

Although the next group that saw the monster also reported seeing a mane, their description varied considerably from that given by the workman on the Glendoe Estate. Fortunately, one of the group was a minister. Ministers, of course, never tell lies—not even about monsters.

The Reverend W. E. Cameron, his wife, and his sister-in-law were vacationing at Loch Ness and stopped at a café near Invermoriston. There were some unfinished meals at one of the tables, but there didn't seem to be anyone around. "Is there anybody home?" the minister finally called out.

"I can't come down now," came a voice from the balcony. "I'm looking at the monster."

The minister and the two women bounded swiftly up the stairs. A group of excited people were lined up on the balcony staring out over the loch.

At first glance, Mrs. Cameron thought she was seeing an overturned boat with its lights on. Then she realized that she was looking at a pair of shining eyes. Others in the group later described the eyes as being circular, large, and glittering.

None of the people had a pair of binoculars and the creature was nearly a thousand yards from them. Nevertheless, they had a fairly good view. Their descriptions were in more or less complete agreement.

Everyone noticed that the monster had two shining eyes and a sort of frill or mane at the top of the neck. There were two dark humps in sight most of the time. Two of the women saw splashing some distance behind the last hump and they assumed that the commotion was caused by the tail. In spite of the distance, they all agreed that the neck was sticking straight out of the water and that the head was not much larger than the neck.

The reporter who spoke to the people at the café got a nice item of added interest. He learned that an employee of the Caledonian Canal had watched the monster for several

74

minutes that very same morning. When interviewing the man, the reporter was puzzled by certain differences in the descriptions. This, though, didn't really disturb him. His job was to report the news, not to interpret it.

It was nine thirty in the morning when the canal employee had spotted the monster. The loch was absolutely calm. Not even a ripple disturbed the water. The creature was roughly five hundred yards from the shore. She remained in sight for several minutes and the observer had studied her closely.

He judged that at least thirty feet of the monster was in clear view. The neck was about five feet long and a foot thick. The head was flatter than the head of a cow, but was approximately the same size and shape. Although the man was unable to see any eyes, the creature was obviously alert, turning its head first in one direction and then in the other. Dark, rough-looking skin covered the great body. When the monster changed course, the observer saw the front paddles working rapidly.

While the man was watching, he heard the sound of a boat coming through the canal. He believed that Nessie had heard it first. She had been trying to determine the source of the noise by swinging her head back and forth. When the sound increased, the monster grew nervous and sank straight down out of sight.

There was no reason to think that the man was playing games with the truth. He was describing the creature as accurately as possible. He had seen it on several other occasions and reported the sightings to the press. This time, however, he asked the newspaperman not to reveal his name. He was getting a bit tired of being teased about the monster.

Why the two descriptions varied was something that couldn't be explained. The people on the café balcony had seen a sort of frill or mane on the back of the monster's neck. They had also noticed a pair of large shining eyes. Why, then, hadn't the canal employee who had been so much closer seen the mane and shining eyes?

But that wasn't all. The man from the canal had declared that the beast's head was approximately the same size and shape as the head of a cow. The café group had agreed that the head was only slightly larger than the neck.

To confuse the issue even more, the reporter remembered that Mrs. Finlay had seen two stalklike projections on the creature's head, but hadn't noticed any eyes. Still another witness had seen two stumps like broken-off sheep's horns and eyes like the slits in darning needles.

The newspaperman shrugged his shoulders and drove back to Inverness to write his story. He was beginning to think that either the loch had monsters to fit every description or else the Loch Ness Monster had a whole series of interchangeable heads.

Chapter **20**

If a scientist attempted to construct a model of the Loch Ness Monster, he would almost certainly end up as a jibbering idiot.

His first job would be to gather together all the available information. This, of course, would include the written and verbal reports of those who had actually seen the creature. Once he had enough material on hand, he would be ready to start building his model of the monster. Most likely, he'd build the body first.

According to eyewitnesses, the monster's body

1. was dark brown,
2. was elephant-gray,
3. was black and shiny,
4. was dark and mottled like a toad's body,
5. was egg-shaped,
6. was like a giant tadpole,
7. was like a giant snail,
8. was like a gigantic eel,
9. was like an elephant's back,

10. was like an upturned boat,
11. was five feet long,
12. was about twenty-five feet long,
13. was at least forty feet long,
14. had no visible humps,
15. had one large hump,
16. had two humps,
17. had seven large angular humps,
18. had nine humps shaped like a roof,
19. had twelve humps,
20. had flippers in front and back,
21. had little paddlelike things in front,
22. had neither paddles nor flippers.

After finishing work on the body, he would probably start on the neck. The scientist would have learned by now that the monster's neck

1. was swanlike,
2. was snakelike,
3. was like a partially submerged telegraph pole,
4. was like a very thick periscope,
5. was exactly like the trunk of an elephant,
6. had a small frill on top,
7. had a curious fin on the back,
8. had something like hair or wool hanging down,
9. had a mane like a horse or lion,
10. was perfectly smooth.

If the scientist wasn't thoroughly confused by this time, he would start work on the model's head. This is the part guaranteed to make him despair. Eyewitness reports would have informed him that the Loch Ness Monster's head

1. was larger than a dog's and definitely snakelike,
2. was like a bird in the water,
3. was like a turtle's head,
4. was like a horse's head,
5. was like a goat's head,
6. was like a camel's head,
7. was like a giraffe's head with the ears missing,
8. was like a cow's head, but flatter,
9. was like a deer's head with little horns,
10. was like a seal's head,
11. was like an eel's head,
12. had large and glittering eyes,
13. had eyes like the slits in darning needles,
14. didn't seem to have any eyes at all,
15. had a mouth, but you could hardly see it,
16. had a big mouth that kept opening and shutting as though it was gasping for breath,
17. had horns like those on a snail,
18. had two stumps like broken-off sheep's horns.

With all this information at hand, it would be very interesting to see what sort of a model of the monster the scientist would finally construct. Chances are, of course, that he'd never really try to make one. He'd give up before he even got started.

Chapter 21

People often ask why the descriptions of the monster vary so much. Well, that can be explained in several different ways. If you had only seen one horse in your life and you had seen it from the back, you would find it very difficult to tell people what a horse looked like.

Now if someone else had seen only one horse and he had seen it from the front, his description would be very different. The person seeing a horse from the side would see it still differently. Then, too, a horse is a horse, but it comes in different shapes, sizes, and colors. The same thing is undoubtedly true of monsters.

It must also be remembered that very few people get a good close look at Nessie. She's usually a few hundred yards away. Sometimes she's shooting around at top speed. Other times she's partly hidden in a shower of spray. More often, only a few dark humps can be seen.

When a person sees the Loch Ness Monster, he's going to get terribly excited. The closer he is to it, the more agitated he's going to get. This is only natural. It's also natural that a person in a state of high excitement is not apt to be a particularly accurate observer. That's because he can hardly see straight.

Here's another difficulty: People who have seen the monster have trouble describing it because it doesn't look like anything they've ever seen before. If Nessie looked like a dog or a frog or a cat or a rat, it would be a simple matter to describe her. But Nessie, unfortunately, just doesn't seem to look like anything else.

Someone once suggested that the Loch Ness Monster might resemble a dugong. This was an interesting suggestion, but it had one serious drawback. Hardly anyone knows what a dugong looks like, either.

There is, of course, one reason why the descriptions vary and that's because people are describing different monsters. It's now generally acknowledged that Nessie is actually a family or a herd of monsters. This would mean that there are old monsters and young monsters in Loch Ness. Enormous monsters and mini-monsters. Monsters with manes like horses and monsters with stalklike projections on their heads. In short, monsters to fit nearly all the descriptions given.

Members of the Loch Ness Phenomena Investigation Bureau soon learned that nearly everyone who has seen the monster has difficulty describing what they have seen. So somebody had a bright idea. If people couldn't describe what they had seen, they could draw a picture of it. Then the bureau members learned something else. They learned that most people can't draw, either.

Although an estimated three thousand people have seen and described the Loch Ness Monster, one of the very earliest descriptions has never been improved upon: "The dreadful beast, the direful wurrum—half fish and half dragon . . ."

Chapter 22

To the early Anglo-Saxons, a worm was more than merely a worm. The name was also applied to serpents and dragons. An ancient Scottish chronicle tells us that "In the parochin of Lintoune ther happen to breed ane hydeous monster in the forme of a Worme, soe called and esteemed by the countrie people."

Another "Worme" in the form of a "hydeous monster" wormed its way into British history. This was the Lambton Worm. The Lambton family is still prominent in Great Britain and is certainly the only family to have a worm named after it.

The legend of the Lambton Worm probably began in the fifteenth century. The Lambtons were an ancient and distinguished family who owned an enormous estate on the river Wear. Not only were they very wealthy, but they were also well educated. In those distant days, anyone who could read and write was thought of as a well-educated person.

Young John Lambton, it seems, was a bit of a rascal. He was the eldest son of a rich and powerful family and was probably spoiled. At any rate, he didn't care what people

82

thought of him. He even shocked the neighborhood by going fishing on Sundays. This was just about as naughty as anyone could be. Even today, it is strictly against the law in Scotland to fish for salmon on Sunday.

But John Lambton couldn't have cared less. He was the heir to the family fortune and he would do as he very well pleased. If he wanted to fish on a Sunday, then he would fish on a Sunday.

His friends and neighbors were shocked and unhappy. A man who fished on the Sabbath was asking for trouble, they whispered to one another. Something terrible was certainly going to happen to him.

One Sunday morning, John hooked what he thought must be an enormous fish. While he was struggling away, two peasants who were on their way to church stopped to watch the fun. After a tough fight, John at last managed to pull his prize ashore. But to his disgust, he hadn't hooked a fish at all. He had caught something resembling a huge, hideous worm. The peasants, however, believed that young John had caught the devil.

The creature's appearance was so hideous that John was filled with loathing. He could hardly stand to look at the beast. Not wishing to throw the worm back into the river, he dragged it over to a nearby well and dumped it in. In later years, this well became known as Worm Well.

As time went by, the worm grew larger and larger and larger. Finally, it managed to escape from its home in the well and made its way back to the river Wear. People sometimes saw the thing on the shore. There was a small hill near the river where the worm also liked to lie. This hill, of course, became known as Worm Hill.

Being an adventurous young man, John left his home and the worm behind and set off on a crusade to the Holy

Land. The next few years were spent traveling and waging war against the heathen Turks. When he finally returned home, the knight found things in a terrible mess.

The worm had gone on the warpath. It was now a prodigiously large and powerful creature. Besides, it had a vile temper. From time to time, it would lash out in anger, killing and destroying.

People lived in a state of perpetual fear. They were afraid to leave their homes and crops rotted in the fields. Old Lord Lambton locked himself and his family inside the castle. The worm was now in complete command.

Something had to be done at once and John decided that he was the man who would have to do it. But how? Several men had already set forth to slay the worm. Things, however, had not gone according to plan. The men were now dead, but the worm was still very much alive.

John went out and had a look at the worm. He wasn't at all happy with what he saw, so he went to get the advice of a local witch. She told him to stud his armor with the tips of spears. When fighting the worm, he was supposed to use the same sword that he had used against the heathen in the Holy Land.

Then the old witch exacted a promise from the knight. No one knows why, but witches can be difficult people to understand. She made the knight vow to kill the first living thing he saw after killing the worm. The knight faithfully promised to do so.

With his armor studded with spear tips and his crusading sword in his hand, John bravely set out to challenge the worm. He found it lying on a large rock in the river.

The battle was a fierce one. Both the knight and the worm fought courageously. The worm, however, seemed to have a slight advantage. It was stronger and faster. With a sudden lunge, it succeeded in getting a coil wrapped around John. Then another coil and still another coil followed. The knight's sword arm was pinned to his side and he thought he was a goner. But as the worm squirmed and tightened its grip, the spear tips ripped its body into shreds. At last it could hang on no longer. It uncoiled and tried to escape. John lunged after it and swung a mighty blow. His sword sliced all the way through the hideous creature and the battle was over.

But John still had to keep the promise he had made to the witch. He had told his father that if he managed to kill the worm, he would sound his hunting horn. His father would then release an old hound. The hound would be the first living thing the knight would see after killing the worm. By killing the dog, he would fulfill his promise to the witch.

When old Lord Lambton heard the blast of the horn, he went wild with joy. The horrible worm was dead! His gallant son had killed it. The hound was forgotten and the old man went tottering out to congratulate his son.

John stopped in his tracks when he saw his father coming toward him. What went wrong? he asked himself. Where's the hound? What am I going to do now? How am I going to keep the vow I made to the old witch?

There was only one thing the knight could do. He laid his sword aside and marched over to the witch's house. The worm was dead, he told her, but something had gone wrong with his plan. The first living thing he had seen after slaying the worm was his father. He admitted that he had vowed to kill the first living thing he saw after killing the worm, but he just couldn't abide the thought of killing his old daddy.

It seems that the witch had a soft spot in her heart for the brave young knight. No harm would come to him for breaking his vow, she promised. Future generations, however, would have to pay the penalty. For the next nine generations,

85

she foretold, no Lord of Lambton would die in his bed.

This prediction seems to have come true. The Lords of Lambton have always had the reputation of being men who died with their boots on.

The story of the worm has, of course, been greatly exaggerated. Legends, however, are very often based on truths. Most likely some strange creature actually was seen in and around the river Wear. The young Lord of Lambton may even have killed it. Peasants in those days frequently attributed seemingly impossible acts of valor to their masters. Killing a worm was nothing to brag about. But if a man killed a giant worm that had been terrorizing the countryside, that was a different matter entirely. Parents would tell the story to their children who, in turn, would tell it to *their* children. The story might grow with each telling, but it would have grown from a grain of truth.

We don't know exactly what kind of a worm it was that caused all this trouble. We can imagine, though, that "the dreadful beast, the direful wurrum—half fish and half dragon" was somehow related to the Loch Ness Monster.

Chapter **23**

People visiting Loch Ness are very apt to see a man lazily drifting around in a boat. A canopy overhead protects him from the sun and the sudden squalls of rain, which are a feature of the Scottish Highlands. It also protects a couple of pairs of binoculars, a couple of still cameras, and a large movie camera fitted with a long telephoto lens. The name of the man in the boat is Tim Dinsdale. No man has ever had a more severe case of monster fever.

As far as is known, there is no cure for monster fever. Aspirins don't help and neither do hot baths. Perhaps the only possible cure would be to get a perfect close-up photograph of Nessie. This is something that Tim Dinsdale has spent thousands of hours trying to do.

It was early in 1960 that Dinsdale came down with his case of monster fever. Up to that time, he had given the matter almost no thought. There happened to be a monster in Loch Ness and that was all there was to it.

But when the fever struck, he became a changed man. Now he could think of little else. He was like a man in love. Nessie was on his mind constantly and he was determined to find out all about her.

Being an engineer, he attacked the problem methodically. He read everything he could find on monsters. Long, questioning letters were sent to people who had seen Nessie. Other letters went off to zoologists, marine biologists, and that curious breed of men known as ichthyologists. Every scrap of information was studied carefully and fitted somewhere into the general pattern. After several months, an image of the monster began to take shape in Dinsdale's mind. He was quite sure that he would recognize Nessie immediately no matter where he saw her.

And now Dinsdale decided on a very strange course of action. He was going to take a week off from work. Counting the two Saturdays and two Sundays, he would have nine free days altogether. It would take him two days to drive from his home in England to Loch Ness and two more days to drive back. He would spend five days at the loch and during that time he would shoot some moving pictures of the monster.

This was a splendid idea. It was like someone saying, "I think I'll climb yonder hill and take a movie of the next flying saucer that comes sailing along."

But the age of miracles is not over. Nor is the age of monsters. On his last day at Loch Ness, Tim Dinsdale spotted Nessie. She was more than halfway across the loch and heading rapidly for the far shore. In spite of the distance, Dinsdale focused the camera he had borrowed and shot fifty feet of movie film. Then he hurried back home to get it developed.

The results were far from encouraging. The film showed the strange humped back of the monster moving through the water at a good speed. The last few feet of film pictured the creature sinking below the surface, then moving down the loch like a small submarine.

Dinsdale had hoped for far more spectacular results, but

88

he wasn't too disappointed. After all, he had successfully photographed a huge living creature in a freshwater lake. Now all he had to do was wait for the world's scientists to beat a path to his front door.

He waited and waited, but no one came. Then he waited some more and still nobody came. This was too much. Surely the zoologists and marine biologists would all be anxious to see his film. The one thing Dinsdale had not expected was a complete lack of interest. All right, he finally decided, if the scientists don't want to see my film, let's see how the general public reacts.

Knowing that the Americans have a reputation for getting things done in a hurry, he took his precious package to a firm of film distributors. The two young Americans he approached swung into immediate action. Almost before Dinsdale could say, "The Loch Ness Monster might be a plesiosaur," a program had been planned.

First of all, his film would be enlarged to four times its present size. Single frames of the film would be rephotographed and the pictures sent to newspapers abroad. An interview would also be arranged with the publisher of one of Britain's leading newspapers. That done, the film would be shown on television and Dinsdale would provide the commentary and later answer questions.

Everything went off exactly as planned. The enlarged version of the film was an enormous success. It even showed a definite paddling action that could not be seen on the original.

Public reaction was highly favorable. The man in the street was very interested in the Loch Ness Monster. Mail piled high on Dinsdale's desk. Some folks were volunteering information and others were asking for it. Many simply

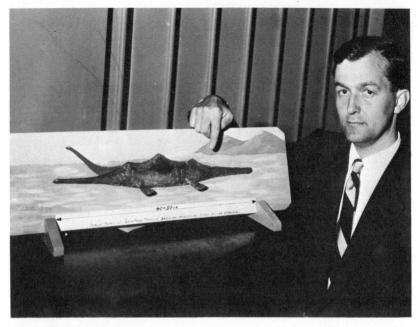

Tim Dinsdale displays a model he made of the monster. (*United Press International*)

wanted to congratulate him on his accomplishment.

Dinsdale was anxious to get all his correspondence out of the way. He was in a hurry to get back to Loch Ness. His ambition now was to get a close-up sequence of the monster.

As this is being written, he's still drifting around in his boat trying to get it.

Chapter 24

One of the few scientists who took a thoroughly active interest in the monster as early as 1960 was Dr. Denys Tucker of Birmingham University. His lectures at Oxford and Cambridge universities aroused so much interest that thirty students volunteered to spend a month of their summer vacation at Loch Ness. Their purpose was to attempt to establish the identity of the Loch Ness Monster.

The expedition's equipment consisted only of cameras and some echo-sounding apparatus. Volunteers stationed themselves up and down both sides of the loch and kept a sharp lookout. The echo-sounding equipment was operated by engineering students who floated silently around the loch in a small boat.

At the end of the month, the findings were summed up. These were the results: One volunteer saw what he thought was the monster's back. Another watched something that appeared to keep changing its shape. The engineering students reported some echo soundings of an unusual nature. And that was it.

The results were disappointing. Thirty volunteers had

spent long hours straining their eyes and had come up with almost nothing. They had, however, proved one thing. Even an organized expedition would need a great stroke of luck to make its mission a success.

The Oxford and Cambridge Expedition was the first attempt made to locate Nessie with echo-sounding equipment. Oddly enough, though, she had been picked up once by an echo sounder, but it had been one of those things that just happened to happen.

Six years earlier, a fishing boat was passing through the loch on its way to a port on the North Sea. A man called Peter Anderson was at the wheel. The rest of the crew were below having lunch.

As Anderson steered, he occasionally glanced at the echo-sounding graph. But suddenly he stared! The chart showed something that had no business being there. Instead of a blank space of water, the chart indicated a vague form somewhere between the bottom of the loch and the surface. It was like nothing Anderson had ever before seen on the graph.

He yelled to the crew to come on deck and take a look. All of them were thoroughly familiar with the echo-sounding equipment. They were fishermen and the apparatus was used to locate shoals of fish. The men studied the graph and shook their heads. This was something completely new to them and they couldn't explain it.

Anderson had to satisfy his curiosity. The boat was turned around and he sailed back and forth over the course he had just covered. Nothing happened and Anderson thought he might now have the answer. The echo sounder had recorded something alive and that something had since moved off.

As they passed through the locks, Anderson kept showing the section of the chart to other fishermen. They were all as mystified as he was. News, of course, soon got out that the

92

echo-sounding equipment on a fishing boat had picked up something unusual in Loch Ness. Before the boat cleared the Caledonian Canal, the deck was crawling with reporters.

It takes a certain amount of experience to be able to interpret all the lines and squiggles on an echo-sounding chart. The newspapermen did not have this experience, but that minor fact didn't discourage them. They brashly declared the vague form to be the Loch Ness Monster.

This wasn't good enough for Anderson. Although he was quite willing to agree that it *might* be the monster, he refused to make a definite statement.

The chart was sent to the firm that had designed and built the equipment. Experts examined the graph and shook their heads. They all agreed that this was a new one on them.

There was no way of knowing just what the vague form represented. It might be one very large creature or it could also be a number of smaller ones swimming nose to tail. Nor was it possible to get an accurate estimate of the size of the object because no one could tell at what speed it had been traveling. The experts would only say that the echo sounder had recorded a shape or shapes of an unknown object either swimming or floating at a depth of four hundred and eighty feet.

Many people were naturally convinced that the unidentified object was none other than Nessie herself. But why wasn't she picked up oftener by the echo-sounders? they asked. After all, well over a thousand vessels pass through Loch Ness every year and the echo-sounding equipment is usually in operation during the passage. Why, then, had she only been picked up the one time?

That question begged another one. With so many vessels passing through the canal each year, why wasn't Nessie seen by the crews from time to time?

There can be only one answer. The noise chases her deep down into the depths or wherever else it is that she goes to hide. People in rowboats and sailboats have sighted Nessie quite frequently. Crews of power-driven vessels almost never see her. Only on very, very rare occasions have they seen her with their eyes or on their echo sounders.

The same thing no doubt applies to the great sea serpent. In the old days of sail, sightings were relatively common. Now that huge piston-driven ships are thumping their noisy way across the seas, the great sea serpent is seldom seen.

Chapter **25**

There are many people living in areas where tigers and leopards are quite plentiful, yet they've never seen one. These animals normally hunt only at night and are seldom seen during the day. The same thing seems to be true of Nessie.

No ships pass through the Caledonian Canal at night and no fishing is permitted on Loch Ness after 8:00 P.M. The nights are long at this latitude and few people are moving about.

What Nessie does at night is anyone's guess. Mr. and Mrs. George Spicer and T. P. Grant saw her on land, so it's known that she occasionally goes for a stroll. How often she goes for a stroll is not known. Neither is it known why she goes for a stroll. She has the loch pretty much to herself after dark and can do as she pleases.

People who have seen Nessie at close range during the day have described her as being a very frightening beast. Those who bumped into her at night found it a terrifying experience. Quite a number of people who have camped by the loch have spent a part of the night in their cars after hearing Nessie splashing about close to the shore.

Thanks to Nessie, there are a few people who will never again break the law by fishing after 8:00 P.M. One of them is a farmer who has always lived near the loch. It was his custom to sneak down to Urquhart Bay after dark and set out a few lines. Before daylight, he would be back at the bay to collect his catch. He often had a couple of trout or salmon and he easily sold those to the tourist hotels.

Early one morning, the poacher came down the hill to the bay. He was approaching one of his lines when he noticed a disturbance in the water. Then he stopped dead in his tracks! Some sort of a huge, dark shape was moving about close to the shore. What could it be? he wondered. Just as he took a cautious step forward, the head and long neck of the monster reared high above the surface of the loch.

The man whirled around and took off at top speed, not slowing down until the loch was well behind him. Never again would he visit the loch during the hours of darkness, he declared emphatically.

On another occasion, Nessie did even better. This time she convinced *three* men that it was very naughty to fish after 8:00 P.M.

The spring salmon run was in full swing and the men from the village of Dores thought that a couple of big fish would look very nice in the freezer. They pushed off in a small boat and headed for Tor Point. Salmon entering the loch from the river Ness had to pass the point and the men were looking forward to some good sport.

It was a beautiful night. The only sound was the gentle lap of the waves against the boat. The fishermen drifted lazily along, casting their flies as they went. But the peaceful scene didn't last. To the men's horror, their little boat was suddenly lifted by some unseen force. It was raised slowly and steadily until it was almost clear of the water. The boat teetered dangerously for a few seconds and the men were certain that it was going to capsize. Then the unseen force lowered them almost gently back to their original position. The water swirled and the three terrified men saw a large shapeless form moving away from them.

It seems that Nessie had also decided to go salmon fishing at Tor Point that night.

Mr. H. L. Cockrell is another man who met the monster at night. Unlike the others, however, Cockrell deliberately set out to look for Nessie—and he set out in a canoe! Perhaps the strangest thing about Cockrell's story is that he lived to tell it.

Like Tim Dinsdale, Cockrell suffered from a bad case of monster fever. He, too, decided that he had to have a picture of Nessie. The best time to take it, he believed, was during the hours of darkness, when the creature was more apt to be feeding.

So each evening Cockrell pushed off from shore in his frail canoe. Although he could handle his craft expertly, Loch Ness is no place for a small boat. More than one has been swamped in a sudden squall. It's not too bad close to shore, but canoeing in the center can be suicidal. Then, too, a canoe is an unlikely craft in which to go monster hunting. Nevertheless, this monster hunter always paddled off soon after dark.

His camera setup was an ingenious one. It was carried on his head and so arranged that it was aimed in the direction he was facing. He had rigged up the flash equipment and shutter mechanism so that he could snap the picture simply by biting down on a little trigger-type affair. This would leave both of his hands free to handle the canoe. Or to beat Nessie over the head with the paddle if she came too close to him.

The last night of Cockrell's hunt was an unusually calm one. There was no breeze. Not a ripple disturbed the surface of the loch. It was lonely, beautiful, and frightening. Clouds crossing the face of the moon cast eerie shadows on the loch's glasslike surface. Each shadow looked like a monster and Cockrell was beginning to wish he were home in bed.

Then he saw something strange! It was about fifty yards away and swimming steadily in his direction. Shadows can't swim and they don't create a wake. The man in the canoe felt a moment of panic. Now he *really* wished that he were home in bed.

As the shape came closer, Cockrell saw what he thought must be a very large flat head. It appeared to be about five feet long and about the same width. It was just above the surface of the water. He realized then that the head was not a head at all, but the back of a very large creature.

The shape kept narrowing the gap and Cockrell was not one bit happy. He was directly in the creature's path, which he thought was a very poor place to be. He had to get out of there and fast! But when he swung swiftly off to one side, the monster also changed course and again came straight at him.

With a supreme effort of will, Cockrell stood his ground. There was no place he could hide anyway, and he certainly couldn't race the creature to the shore. There was only one thing he could do and that was what had brought him out on the loch at night in the first place.

But Nessie had tired of her little game. Just as Cockrell was clenching his teeth to snap the picture, she suddenly sank like a stone. All, however, was not lost. The photograph showed a large dark shape disappearing in a concentric circle of waves.

Although it was actually a rather poor photograph, Cockrell was very happy. Not because of the photograph, but because he would never have to go through an experience like that again.

Chapter **26**

In spite of the poor results of the Cambridge and Oxford Expedition, two very exciting events occurred during the summer of 1960. The Loch Ness Monster was seen on land during the day and in the second instance a close-up photograph was taken.

The man who saw the monster on shore insisted upon remaining anonymous. He willingly cooperated with reporters, but refused to permit them to use his name.

His position in the community was a highly respected one. There were still cynics who scoffed at those who claimed to have seen the monster and the man could not afford to appear ridiculous. Normally, reports by witnesses who insist upon remaining anonymous are regarded as unreliable. In this case, however, the witness's report was unquestioned.

It was late in the afternoon when the man glimpsed a large grayish-black mass at the extreme west end of Loch Ness. There was a certain something about it that aroused his curiosity. Stopping his car, he got out and studied the object through a pair of powerful binoculars. As he had suspected, the object was alive.

As mentioned earlier, the great majority of witnesses find it difficult to describe what they have seen. Fortunately, this witness was a competent and accurate observer. He also had a one-inch-to-the-mile ordnance map with him, so he was able to pinpoint his own position as well as the monster's. From that information, he was able to compute the distance accurately. Knowing the distance, it was possible for him to establish the creature's size by using the reticulation scale on his binoculars.

The animal was on a steep slope. Its tail and extreme hindquarters were in the water and could not be seen. It took a minute or two for the observer to realize this. The huge creature was so outlandish in appearance that he had at first mistaken the long neck for the tail. Even when he realized his error, he was still unable to distinguish the head. This isn't too surprising. Many witnesses have stated that Nessie's head seems to be no larger than her neck and from a distance is almost impossible to distinguish.

There were paddles, or flippers, both in front and in back. The rear paddles were enormous and obviously very powerful. Because the creature was resting on its front flippers, the man was only able to get a quick look at them when the monster flopped back into the water.

After returning home, the witness did some paper work. He learned that the monster had been almost exactly a mile away from him. He had already measured the reticulation scale on his binoculars. With that information, he was able to establish the length of that part of the monster that was out of the water.

The result was astounding! The *visible* part of the monster was approximately fifty-five feet long. Its overall length, then, would probably be in the neighborhood of seventy feet.

And that, everyone will agree, is an awful lot of monster.

Considerable interest was aroused by the witness's sketch of the Loch Ness Monster. Because he had seen it at a great distance and because he hadn't seen all of it, a certain amount of guesswork was involved. The man emphasized the fact that his sketch showed only what he *thought* the creature looked like.

People who were serious students of the monster were greatly intrigued. The creature on the sketch vaguely resembled a plesiosaur, which is sort of like a seagoing dinosaur. Plesiosaurs had a long neck, a small head, and all four limbs developed as paddles for swimming. They had also been extinct for seventy million years.

So now what? people wanted to know. Well, if the Loch Ness Monster couldn't possibly be a plesiosaur, then it had to be something else. Something else, however, would have to be a completely unknown species of animal.

A couple of months later, students of the monster thought that their problem might at long last be solved. Peter O'Connor, a young member of the Northern Naturalists Association, had managed to get a close-up photograph of the Loch Ness Monster. Perhaps this was it!

O'Connor had come to Loch Ness for the express purpose of seeing the monster. Luck had been on his side all the way. Shortly after his arrival in the Scottish Highlands, he had watched the monster for ten minutes through binoculars from the lawn of the Foyers Hotel. Three residents of Foyers's were also witnesses. These three people had lived on the loch for many years, but had never seen their famous monster. One of them, in fact, had always insisted that Nessie was simply a gimmick dreamed up by hoteliers to attract tourists to the loch.

The first time he saw the monster, O'Connor saw only a dark-brown hump. The great size of the hump surprised him. It indicated a creature much larger than he had expected to see. The sun was hot that afternoon and Nessie appeared to be taking a sunbath. There was no movement at all until she sank slowly into the depths.

Three days later, O'Connor again saw the monster. He was camped a mile from Foyers Bay. About six o'clock that morning, he left his tent and strolled off to find Nessie. Before he had gone a hundred yards, he saw her paddling in his general direction.

Foyers Bay is one of the few places on Loch Ness where the water is shallow close to shore. A rock shelf extends about thirty yards out into the loch. Then it ends abruptly and the water is suddenly hundreds of feet deep. O'Connor saw that if Nessie continued on her present course, she would be out of range of his inexpensive camera. He hesitated a moment, then waded out until the water was up to his waist.

The young naturalist was perhaps more brash than brave. Nessie paddled closer and closer, but O'Connor defiantly stood his ground. He had the horrible feeling that the monster knew he was there. At one point, she turned her head in his direction, and he was terribly tempted to run for cover.

Nessie approached like a giant swan and O'Connor had a chance to study her closely. The head had small sheeplike features and was about ten inches long. He didn't see the eyes, but he believed that they were there. The neck was very powerful. It was about seven inches in diameter and about three feet of it was visible. A large grayish-black rounded hump was all he could see of the body. The tail couldn't be seen, but swirls of water indicated a paddling action of some type.

O'Connor waited motionlessly until the monster was less than twenty-five yards from him. Then he raised his little flash

102

camera and snapped a picture. As soon as the bulb flashed, he yelled to his friend who was still asleep in the tent.

Either the flash or the yell, or both, frightened Nessie and she went down in a shower of foam. O'Connor shot one more picture before she disappeared. His friend came rushing out of the tent just in time to see a dark shape dive into the depths.

Unfortunately, Peter O'Connor's two photographs left very much to be desired. His camera was the kind that can be bought in almost any drugstore for a few dollars. It's all right for taking pictures of people on bright and sunny days, but it's not much good for snapping early-morning photographs of monsters. The camera simply hadn't been designed for such a thing.

In his excitement, the young photographer had completely forgotten to adjust the settings on his camera. He had set them for bright sunshine the previous day and that's where they had stayed. As a result, his photographs of the monster were terribly underexposed.

There's no doubt that extreme nervousness also accounted for the unfortunate results. O'Connor was standing in waist-deep water. The monster was only twenty-five yards from him. He was desperately anxious to shoot his pictures and get out of there fast. As a consequence, he held his camera at an angle and aimed too far to one side. The flash bounced off the rear of the monster's back. The head, neck, and forequarters were so badly underexposed that detail was completely lacking. No one can really blame Peter O'Connor for his poor photography. The most surprising thing is that he actually did manage to get a picture. After all, he waited until the Loch Ness Monster was practically in his lap before he clicked the shutter.

Although O'Connor failed to get a decent photograph,

his experience did prove one thing. It proved that it was possible to get a close-up photograph of Nessie.

A lot of patience and a great deal of luck will be needed, but someday someone with a decent camera is going to snap a perfect photograph of the elusive Loch Ness Monster. It's the sort of thing that might happen at any moment.

Chapter 27

In spite of the fact that Nessie is extremely shy, she has become one of Scotland's most important tourist attractions. During the summer months, traffic around Loch Ness is practically bumper to bumper. The scenery is spectacularly beautiful, but most people don't even see it. They're all trying to catch a glimpse of the monster. The desperate desire of people to see Nessie has led to some amusing incidents.

Andy Hanna, a photographer for the *Scottish Daily Express,* was driving slowly along the loch one evening. The sun was just going down and he decided to take a photograph of the sunset over Urquhart Castle. He parked his car on the side of the road, set up his tripod and squinted through the viewfinder. Before he could snap his picture, bedlam broke loose.

Brakes screeched, car doors were flung open, and people eagerly clutching cameras raced up to Andy's side. "Where is it?" they demanded, their voices shrill with excitement. "Where's the monster?"

When Andy calmly explained that he was merely photographing the sunset, the tourists stamped angrily back to their cars. All of them felt terribly cheated.

Nessie's attraction for tourists has merited a postcard in her honor. (*New York Public Library*)

Some Inverness teen-agers keep themselves amused in summer by tormenting the tourists. Their favorite trick is to stop with their car at a point overlooking a broad expanse of the loch. When a tour bus comes along, they point out over the water and hop about in great excitement. The bus grinds to a sudden stop. The door opens and the tourists come pouring out, cameras at the ready. Then the practical jokers get back in their car and speed away, feeling very pleased with themselves.

People who are extremely anxious to see something are often able to convince themselves that they actually *have* seen it. This is especially true at Loch Ness. The loch is a strange place and many occurrences are difficult to explain. The wake of a boat, for example, can sometimes be seen long after the boat has passed out of sight. A sudden gust of wind will often

106

create an effect similar to a boat's wake. Witnesses see the disturbance in the water and the reason for it is immediately clear. The monster is speeding off to an appointment somewhere and she's causing the wake.

During the tourist season at Loch Ness, every shadow on the water, every object floating in the loch, becomes one of the monster's humps. In one case, three separate humps were seen. An excited crowd gathered. Although the distance was great, cameras clicked furiously. Those fortunate enough to have binoculars confirmed the fact that there were indeed three enormous humps separated by several feet of water. The wake showed that the monster was traveling away from them.

While the crowd watched in great excitement, something entirely unexpected happened. The first hump suddenly took wing and flew off in the general direction of Achnahannet. The other two humps followed almost immediately. People smiled sheepishly at one another, hung their cameras over their shoulders, and silently stole away.

One practical joker single-handedly caused a serious traffic jam on the road around the loch. He dragged an old leather sofa up to the edge of a cliff and shoved it over the side. Since nobody expected to see a sofa floating around in Loch Ness, they all decided that it was the monster.

Their error is understandable. The dark leather was easily mistaken for the monster's hide. Many witnesses had stated that the hump was angular in shape. The sofa was floating in such a position that the appearance was definitely angular. It seemed to be about five or six feet long and that, too, fit in with what some witnesses had reported. Everyone was quite certain that the object was the monster basking in the sun.

The crowd on the northern shore could see that another crowd had gathered on the shore opposite. They could also see two men in a boat. They had pushed off from Temple Pier and were rowing rapidly toward what they assumed was Nessie.

The boat got closer and closer. The crowd stirred uneasily. The men were getting much too close for comfort, but they rowed on and on. At last they were right alongside the "monster." This was asking for trouble and the crowd held its breath. One of the men stood up in the boat, hopped onto the "monster's" back, and gaily waved his white handkerchief at the staring crowds.

Nessie assumes many shapes and the Highlanders themselves have sometimes been fooled. After a violent storm, one of the men living near the loch saw what he thought was a boat floating in an upside-down position. Someone must have capsized during the storm, he thought sadly. His own boat was tied up at the pier and he decided to row out and investigate.

But when he reached the pier, he found a group of excited people. All of them were watching the "Loch Ness Monster." Only one large dark hump was visible and it looked very much like an upturned boat.

In another instance, Nessie was the one who did the fooling. An Inverness police sergeant was wading along the shore casting for trout. It was that time of the evening when it was neither light nor dark. The trout were just beginning to feed. They were rising all around and the sergeant was all set for a strike.

While casting, he glanced out across the loch. A man standing up in a boat was coming rapidly toward him. An angler hates to be disturbed when the trout are feeding and the sergeant was thoroughly annoyed. If the man didn't change course soon, the fishing would be ruined.

The sergeant was about to shout at the man not to come any closer when he got the fright of his life. His visitor was not a man standing up in a boat! It was a pillarlike neck sticking about six feet above the water's surface. The boat was a body approximately twenty-five feet long.

Fishing was forgotten. The policeman made a mad dash for the bank. The sudden splashing startled poor Nessie and she went down in a foaming shower.

Chapter 28

Guests at the Foyers Hotel frequently mention the fact that Nessie has been seen from there on many different occasions.

The manager's explanation is always the same. "Well, this is the widest part of the loch, you see," he tells them, "and it's easier for the monster to turn around here."

This is a typical attitude. The outsiders' interest in the monster is a constant source of amusement to the Highlanders. Bartenders, waiters, and reception clerks are asked thousands of questions during the tourist season. They answer them good-naturedly. Although they get bored by the constant bombardment of questions, they accept it as part of the job.

The beginning of July always brings a flood of tourists to the Scottish Highlands. The overwhelming majority of them are hoping to get a look at the fabulous Loch Ness Monster. Vacationers flock to the north in such numbers that the *Inverness Courier* once issued a solemn warning to the loch's famous inhabitant. LOOK OUT, NESSIE! it headlined. HERE COME THE TOURISTS!

Most Highlanders take their monster rather matter-offactly. They like Nessie and they're sort of proud of her. It pleases them that she's a resident of their loch. She's usually well behaved and she doesn't cost them any money.

And, of course, she's a constant source of amusement. The Highlanders love to joke about Nessie and they smile good-humoredly at tourists who have come halfway around the world to see her. Nevertheless, people in the Highlands do wish that they knew what sort of a creature was living in their loch.

They found the scientists' initial lack of interest difficult to understand. The scientific world just didn't seem to give a hoot about their monster. A zoologist who had never even seen Loch Ness wrote a series of articles for a daily newspaper. He concluded that it was ridiculous to suppose that a large unidentified creature was resident in the loch. A Dutch biologist declared that Nessie was a great sea serpent. An American naturalist said he thought the Loch Ness Monster might be a giant squid. Neither of these two men, however, had visited the Highlands and they were merely making wild guesses.

It was in the spring of 1962 that two British naturalists approached a member of Parliament named David James. They suggested that he use his influence to get the government to finance an expedition to Loch Ness. The purpose of the expedition would be to solve the problem of the Loch Ness Monster for once and always.   ꞏ ꞏ cop. |

James laughed and laughed. He had been brought up in the Scottish Highlands and had always looked upon Nessie as a bit of a joke. As far as he was concerned, there was no problem to solve because there was no monster in Loch Ness. But that wasn't all. A member of Parliament is the British equivalent of an American congressman. If James stood up in the House of Parliament and talked about monsters, everyone

111

would think that he had rocks in his head. He wasn't one bit interested in making himself an object of ridicule.

The naturalists, however, were persistent. They reminded the member of Parliament that Nessie had been making world headlines for nearly thirty years. She had also become big business. Millions of people were intrigued by the mysterious inhabitant of Loch Ness and the time had come to solve the problem. Private expeditions had been unable to identify the monster, so now it was the government's turn to try.

Although his visitors were sincere and intelligent men, James found it difficult to take their request seriously. Governments simply didn't sponsor monster hunts. Nessie may have been a British citizen, but the British government had more important things to do. Trouble was brewing in Northern Ireland, the Middle East, and Southern Africa. Prices were going up fast and wages were going up even faster. Labor disputes were a problem and so was unemployment. The population explosion, pollution, and the Communists were also a problem. Politicians had so many problems, in fact, that they wouldn't have a moment's time for Nessie.

In spite of all the pressing problems, David James was reluctant to give the two naturalists a flat refusal. He promised to look into the matter of the monster and let them know his decision.

The member of Parliament couldn't have known it at the time, but the Loch Ness Monster was destined to become one of the most important things in his life.

Chapter **29**

David James is not a scientist. He is, however, a very practical and dedicated man. When he promised to look into the matter of the monster, he fully intended to take a good hard look into the matter. He did just exactly that and the things he learned amazed him.

Like every other Scottish Highlander, James had heard many tales about the monster in Loch Ness. He refused to take them seriously, however. Nessie was an amusing topic of conversation and nothing more. She didn't exist because she couldn't exist. Nevertheless, he had made a promise to the two naturalists and that promise had to be kept.

The politician's investigations led to some startling discoveries. There was much more to the stories than he had imagined. The Loch Ness Monster had been seen by many hundreds of reliable people. She was not a joke or a figment of someone's imagination. She was an honest-to-goodness monster.

James scratched his head and plunged more deeply into his investigation. He read everything that had ever been written on Nessie. He corresponded with eyewitnesses and questioned scientists. Then he scratched his head some more.

The reports of eyewitnesses could not be ignored. Monks at Saint Benedict's Abbey had seen the creature and so had several ministers of religion. It had also been seen by doctors, lawyers, businessmen, engineers, teachers, and people from practically every other walk of life. Certainly nobody would dare to accuse all of these people of being liars or crackpots. Nor could anyone accuse them of being victims of an optical illusion or a mass hallucination.

It was the reports of the local Highlanders, however, that James found most interesting. These were his people and he knew them well. He knew, too, that those who said they had seen the monster were certain to be ridiculed. Yet woodsmen, farmers, game wardens, shepherds, and others living in the area had all reported sightings. The fact that they were willing to risk ridicule was highly significant. But how many people had seen the monster and not reported it? James wondered. There were certainly many people who would rather keep silent than be laughed at.

The idea of the Loch Ness Monster being a hoax was quickly discarded. It would take a genius to construct a creature that could walk on land, swim at terrific speeds, splash about in a sea of spray, sink vertically, or dive swiftly out of sight.

A hoaxer would also have had to construct a number of different models of the monster to fit all the descriptions. It would be necessary, too, to have a place to hide his inventions and keep them in running order. If the monster was a hoax, then the hoaxer was a mechanical genius with unlimited time, energy, money, and cunning.

Neither could David James believe that the monster was a tourist gimmick. Saint Columba certainly hadn't been promoting tourism when he reported seeing a monster in the water Ness in the sixth century. The man who described Nes-

114

sie as "a direful wurrum" didn't own a travel agency and didn't care about tourists. The witness who claimed to have seen a terrible beast come out of the water and kill three men with three strokes of its tail was definitely not trying to lure visitors to Loch Ness.

The story was the same in later years. Nessie made the headlines constantly when the new road was built along the loch. Although she was seen by dozens of people, it's doubtful that anyone came to Loch Ness to look for her. Times were hard during those years and very few people could afford to travel. Tourists were almost unknown at the loch and there were no hotels where they could spend the night.

During the course of his investigation, James learned that some hotel managers refused to use the monster to attract visitors. Employees at the new Clansman Hotel, for example, watched Nessie for several minutes one afternoon. The hotel was not due to open officially until the following day and the manager asked the staff not to mention the sighting. He was afraid that people would think it was merely a publicity stunt.

Word, of course, leaked out and the manager got some dirty looks from the other hoteliers. They were sure that the whole thing was a clever plot to lure visitors to the Clansman. A few weeks later, they had reason to believe that Nessie had appointed herself as the Clansman Hotel's personal tourist attraction.

Bert MacDonald, a young Highlander, was serving tea in the lounge. He had just set down a tray when he noticed something break through the surface of the loch. It was a calm day; the visibility was perfect. While MacDonald stood and stared, the creature started swimming straight toward the hotel.

The waiter didn't know what to do. There was an elderly American couple and three ladies from Inverness in the lounge. There were also about a dozen English tourists who had come in for tea. MacDonald was certain that the Inverness ladies and the American couple would enjoy seeing the monster, but he was afraid to disturb the English guests.

Teatime is a sacred time for the English. Once their cup of tea has been poured, they withdraw into their own little world. They permit absolutely nothing to come between them and their cup of tea. The earth may quake, bombs may fall, flood or fire may threaten them, but their tea must be drunk before they dash for safety.

MacDonald was a nervous wreck. The creature was coming closer and closer. Forcing himself to be calm, he went over to the table where the Americans were seated. "If you come to the window," he told them, "you'll be able to see the Loch Ness Monster."

"The Loch Ness Monster!" screeched the woman. Then she demanded, "Are you kidding?"

The three ladies from Inverness were told next and they joined the American couple at the window. Nessie was now less than a quarter of a mile away. "The Loch Ness Monster!" one of the ladies called out to the English tourists. "It's coming right toward us!"

It was not an easy decision to make. The tea was scalding hot. If they gulped it down, they would burn themselves painfully. If they left it on the table, it might get cold and not taste too good when they got back. Then one of the older Englishmen had an idea. Picking up his cup and saucer, he marched carefully up to the people staring out of the window.

Nessie approached at an even speed. Her head and neck were below the surface, but two large humps could be seen clearly. The guests agreed that the visible length was roughly thirty feet. Rhythmic splashes were observed on both sides of the front hump and the observers believed that the splashes were caused by paddles, or flippers.

116

The creature was in sight for about six minutes. It kept on a straight course until it was within a hundred yards of the shore. Then it turned off to the right and disappeared behind a line of trees.

All of the witnesses were absolutely convinced that they had seen a very large living creature. The ladies from Inverness were particularly impressed by their experience. Although they had read about the monster on hundreds of occasions, they had never really expected to see it. They also admitted that they had never been entirely convinced that an enormous unidentified creature actually existed in Loch Ness.

The American couple confessed that they had always thought of the Loch Ness Monster as something belonging to the same world as pink elephants and little green men. The English tourists were so thrilled that they even forgave Nessie for disturbing them at teatime.

Chapter **30**

To get more firsthand information on the subject, David James journeyed up to Loch Ness. Several of the monks at the Benedictine Abbey in Fort Augustus were students of the monster, so he checked in at the Abbey Guest House.

Perhaps the politician wasn't aware of it, but his investigation was bringing on an acute attack of monster fever. Like Cockrell, Dinsdale, Mountain, and a few others, he found that Nessie was on his mind at all times. His fondest wish was to get a good close look at her and then determine where she belonged in the animal kingdom.

Being a Highlander himself, James was able to get the close cooperation of the local inhabitants. They were, in fact, anxious to do everything they could to help solve the mystery of the monster. Nessie was a part of their community and they were pleased that a well-known Highland personality had come to the loch to gather information.

Finding eyewitnesses was no problem at all. Monks at the abbey had seen the creature a number of times. They had also recorded the reports of others who had seen her. But as James had suspected earlier, a great number of sightings had

118

never been reported. As his investigation progressed, he learned that the overwhelming majority of people living on the loch had seen the monster at one time or another.

And these were honest and reliable countryfolk. They were not seeking publicity; they were risking ridicule by trying to be helpful. People who had never seen the monster were still inclined to scoff at those who claimed they had seen it.

Although all of the reports were interesting, several of them were truly spectacular. In one instance, children at Drumnadrochit had arrived at school in a state of high excitement. They told their teacher that they had seen a great big horrible animal in the bushy swamp near Urquhart Bay.

There were pictures of prehistoric animals on the classroom wall and the teacher asked them whether the creature they had seen resembled any of the animals on the charts. Without exception, the children pointed to the plesiosaur. The teacher could only shrug his shoulders. A legend printed below the picture stated that the plesiosaur had been extinct for over seventy million years.

The children at Drumnadrochit were not the only ones who declared that the monster closely resembled a plesiosaur. Alex Campbell, water bailiff at Fort Augustus, had lived on the loch for over forty years. During that time, he had seen the creature on seven different occasions. Only once, however, did he get a good look at it from close range.

It was very early on a June morning when Campbell left his cottage on the bank of the loch. He was watching the mist rise when he noticed a slight disturbance in the water. To his utter amazement, an enormous creature rose from the depths. "It was like a monster of prehistoric times," he later told reporters.

The monster had a long, sinuous neck and a flat, snake-

119

like head that was raised six feet above the surface. The body was like a giant camel's hump and Campbell estimated its length at thirty feet. He watched the beast for several minutes before it lowered its neck and dived out of sight.

One of the men who interviewed Alex Campbell brought along a chart showing pictures of prehistoric animals. The water bailiff glanced at the chart and immediately pointed to a member of the plesiosaur family. "That's it!" he exclaimed. "That's the thing I saw!"

Shortly before David James arrived at Loch Ness, Mr. and Mrs. Lowrie and their four sons were out on the loch in their yacht. It was a sunny day and the water was perfectly calm. Mrs. Lowrie prepared lunch and everyone except the youngest boy went below to eat.

The family had just sat down to lunch when the boy who had remained on deck rushed into the cabin. "There's something following us!" he announced in wide-eyed excitement. "Something big and funny!"

All of them hurried to the rear of the yacht. Some sort of strange creature was slicing through the water behind them. An enormous hump rose several feet above the surface. Mr. Lowrie guessed the total length to be more than twice the size of their twenty-six-foot yacht.

The distance between the hump and the boat closed steadily. It almost seemed as though the monster was playing some sort of game. But a game with the monster was the last thing Mrs. Lowrie wanted. Her four children were on board and she was completely terrified. "Let's get out of here," she begged her husband. "That thing could smash us to pieces."

Mr. Lowrie obediently veered hard to the left. Nessie also veered hard to the left and swam up even closer. She was now no more than twenty yards from the yacht. For the next ten minutes, she swam peacefully alongside her new playmate.

120

Her new playmate didn't seem to be very playful, so Nessie finally gave up the game and sank out of sight.

David James mulled over this report and over all the others he had heard about and read about. His monster fever had grown progressively worse and he knew it. He knew, too, that he would not recover until he had solved the mystery of the loch.

After giving Nessie a great deal of thought, James decided not to ask the British government to finance the cost of an expedition to identify her. His monster fever had gotten so bad that he had decided to launch his own expedition.

Chapter 31

The Loch Ness Phenomena Investigation Bureau was formed in 1962. It is still going strong and will most likely keep going that way until Nessie's identity has been established. David James and the two naturalists who first got him interested in the Loch Ness Monster are directors of the organization.

Phenomena is the plural form of phenomenon. The plural is used because more than one phenomenon has been seen in Loch Ness. The dictionary describes a phenomenon as an exceptional or abnormal thing. Nessie may not be abnormal, but she certainly is something exceptional.

It was David James who selected the name for his organization. He feels that it is very undignified to refer to Nessie as a monster. Those who wanted to call the new organization the Loch Ness Monster Investigation Bureau were quickly outvoted.

The first expedition to Loch Ness was a rather sad one. Twenty-two of the twenty-four bureau members who made the trip were only along for the laughs. They thought that the whole venture was a big joke. There was no monster in the loch, but the Scottish Highlands was a pleasant place to spend a couple of weeks.

The next three expeditions were not much more successful than the first, but a great deal of interest had been generated. Young people from many corners of the world came to Loch Ness and acted as volunteer monster watchers. They lived in house trailers on the shore of the loch and everyone had a fine time.

Volunteers worked long hours. They were usually at their stations by first light and stayed there until late in the evening. Binoculars and cameras with telephoto lenses were always at the ready. Although monster watching wasn't a strenuous job, it could be a very uncomfortable one. The Scottish Highlands can get terribly cold and wet even during the months of summer. A cold and wet monster watcher is very apt to become a highly disgruntled monster watcher.

Then David James stumbled upon something that made the volunteers' lives much more sunny and pleasant. A careful study of past sightings showed that 97 percent of them had been made on hot sunny days when the loch had been as calm as a mirror. Nessie, it seemed, hated bad weather.

This was wonderful news! It meant that the volunteers would not have to do any monster watching when the weather was bad. They would be free to trek in the hills, go horseback riding, or anything else they cared to do. Their days of sitting out in the cold and wet were over. Morale skyrocketed and everyone was happy.

Well, *almost* everyone was happy. The directors of the organization tried to keep smiling, but they had a couple of rather serious problems.

The biggest problem, of course, was Nessie herself. She absolutely refused to cooperate with the monster watchers. Although tourists and local inhabitants reported sightings

123

from time to time, bureau members kept drawing blanks. "The year 1964 was operationally a failure," mourned David James. "There were only two decent sightings in 1965, and in 1966 Nessie again eluded our cameras."

This was indeed a sorry kettle of fish. Volunteers had spent more than ten thousand man-hours scanning the loch. Tens of thousands of dollars had been spent and still very little had been accomplished.

And that was the other serious problem. Money! Powerful binoculars and cameras with long-range telephoto lenses are expensive items. So are house trailers, motorboats, and the vehicles needed to transport volunteers to their stations around the loch. All these things cost money and money was almost as hard to find as the monster.

The future of the Loch Ness Phenomena Investigation Bureau was looking awfully bleak, but it suddenly received a faint glimmer of hope. Dr. Roy Mackal, a professor at the University of Chicago, stopped to visit the bureau headquarters at Achnahannet one day. He asked a lot of questions and spent considerable time studying the information posted on bulletin boards in the office.

The next day he came back and did the same thing. On the third day he was back again. The volunteers looked at one another and smiled sympathetically. They knew that the professor had caught monster fever.

Dr. Mackal stopped in London on his way back home and introduced himself to David James. Both men were passionately interested in Nessie and spent several happy hours discussing her. During the course of the conversation, James mentioned the bureau's financial difficulties. Unless the directors were able to raise some money, he said, they would not be able to stay in operation.

The American professor smiled. Chicago was a wealthy

124

city and many people there were interested in the Loch Ness Monster. Dr. Mackal believed that it would be easy to raise enough money to enable the Loch Ness Phenomena Investigation Bureau to continue its search.

Chapter 32

The letter from Dr. Mackal was a disappointing one. He had been unable to raise any money at all. When he told people why the money was needed, they smilingly slammed the door in his face. But there were a few who didn't smile. These people slapped their knees and laughed aloud. "The Loch Ness Monster! Ha, ha, ha."

This didn't mean, of course, that people weren't interested in the monster. They were. They were also interested in ghosts, dwarfs, elves, and mermaids, but they weren't going to give them any money.

Although the sad news came as a cruel blow, it was more or less what David James had expected. He could easily remember when he, too, had scoffed at the monster and seriously questioned its existence. The people in Chicago could hardly be blamed for their cynical attitude. They had no positive proof that a monster lived in Loch Ness. Why, then, should they contribute money to identify something that might be no more than a myth?

A short time after sending his letter, Dr. Mackal sent James a telegram. It was an invitation to come to the United States to address the Chicago Adventurers' Club.

126

Most of the members of the Chicago Adventurers' Club were wealthy and successful businessmen. They were also practical and hardheaded. If their visitor could give them proof that there was a monster in Loch Ness, then they would believe him. If not—well, it would at least be amusing to hear what he had to say.

The club members listened to what David James had to say and they listened with open mouths. Everything about their guest surprised them. He was far from being a dreamer or a crackpot, as they had first supposed. Like themselves, he was a successful, practical, and hardheaded businessman. He was also a Scottish laird and a member of the British Parliament. His intelligence and sincerity could not be doubted. Neither could his unshakable belief in the existence of the Loch Ness Monster be doubted.

James's speech to the Chicago Adventurers' Club was a howling success. It was so successful, in fact, that he left Chicago with a big fat check in his pocket. The Loch Ness Phenomena Investigation Bureau had been saved. Members could continue their search for Nessie.

There were also several new members who would be coming to Loch Ness the following summer to serve as volunteer monster watchers. The new members had been recruited from the Chicago Adventurers' Club.

Chapter **33**

Things at the Achnahannet Bureau Headquarters were looking more cheerful. Freshly painted green trucks and house
trailers stood in neat rows. A couple of new green boats were
tied up at the pier. Extra camera equipment had been pur-
chased. The Monster Display in the office trailer was all in
order and there was money in the bank. Much of this had
been made possible by a generous gift from Chicago's Field
Enterprises Educational Corporation.

Over twenty-five thousand people paid a quarter each to
visit the Monster Display at Achnahannet that summer. Bulletin boards in the trailer gave as much information as possible
about Nessie. Sightings had been plotted on a large map of
the loch. There were also diagrams of prehistoric monsters
that might have resembled the loch's present inhabitant.

The attitude of visitors had changed greatly. At first,
people had laughed and scoffed at the monster watchers. Now
they were genuinely interested in what was going on. Intelligent questions were asked and bureau members were pleased
by the intellectual curiosity shown. Cynics were beginning to
realize that there actually was something to this Loch Ness

A poster describing the activities of the Loch Ness Phenomena Investigation Bureau.

Monster business. Serious and dedicated people were making every effort to solve the mystery of the loch.

One of the visitors to bureau headquarters created a sudden flurry of high excitement. He had spent thirty years in the British army and retired as a colonel. While a soldier, he had traveled in many strange lands and learned many strange things. One of the strangest things he had learned was the art of divining. This meant that he was able to find things that no one else was able to find. "Just give me a few minutes," he told the volunteers, "and I'll show you exactly where your monster is hiding."

The colonel unfolded a map of Loch Ness and spread it out on a table. He then placed a T-shaped object in the center of the map. Something resembling a large needle hung by a thread from one arm of the T. "This is my pendulum," he explained to the eager audience crowded around the table. "It gives me a reaction, you see."

A slight flip of a finger set the arm of the T into motion. It revolved slowly. The needle swung back and forth on the thread. As soon as the pendulum came to rest, the monster diviner made a small cross on his map. The same thing was done several more times.

"Now"—he smiled, adjusting his monocle and smoothing his mustache—"we're all set. I simply connect the mark at the bottom with the mark at the top; the one on the left with the one on the right. We'll find the monster where the lines intersect."

There was a hushed and expectant silence. It was a moment of magic. The volunteers leaned anxiously over the table. They were almost afraid to breathe. The top and the bottom marks were joined. Then a line was drawn from the left mark to the right one. The silence was broken by an an-

130

guished moan. The two lines met on a hilltop four miles west of the loch.

"Well, what do you suppose Nessie is doing way up there?" a volunteer wanted to know.

The monster diviner gave everyone a big smile. "I'm afraid the pendulum indicated a mineral reaction," he explained, polishing his monocle. "There must be uranium or gold or something like that on the hill, you see."

After erasing the old marks, he replaced his monocle and had another try. There was another anguished moan when the two lines intersected in downtown Drumnadrochit. The third attempt was no more successful than the first two efforts. That one showed Nessie strolling through the heavy tourist traffic between Invermoriston and Inverfarigaig. "How that little girl does get around!" a bureau member exclaimed wryly.

The other volunteers were too disappointed to be amused. Their faith in the monster diviner had been completely crushed.

But the colonel had a perfect excuse for his failure to find Nessie. "There is no monster in Loch Ness," he firmly declared. "If there *were* a monster in the loch, I would have divined it."

"And if there isn't a monster in the loch, what do you think we're doing here?" one of the female members inquired gently.

"That's easy." The monster diviner smiled at the girl while smoothing his mustache. "I think you're wasting your time. That's what I think you're doing here." Then he folded his map, put the T-shaped object into his briefcase, and silently stole away to divine somewhere else.

"Better luck next time," muttered a disappointed member of the Loch Ness Phenomena Investigation Bureau.

131

Chapter 34

A four and a half page article in the *Reader's Digest* helped to make the Loch Ness Monster the world's most famous mystery.

People were amused, intrigued, and completely baffled. What can it be? they asked. What sort of a creature is it? What does it look like? How large is it? Is it dangerous? What's it doing in Loch Ness? Is it a dragon? Is it a plesiosaur? Is it a sea cow? Or a sea lion? Or a sea serpent? Or what?

Directors of the Loch Ness Phenomena Investigation Bureau and Holly Arnold, their American secretary, were up to their armpits in mail. It came in big batches and it came from all over the world. Bureau membership shot up and tens of thousands of people visited the Monster Display at Achnahannet.

And what was Nessie doing all this time? Well, she was behaving in her usual mysterious manner. Somehow or another, she was remarkably successful in avoiding the cameras of the monster watchers stationed around the loch. Nobody knows how she did it, but she almost always managed to appear in an area where there were no bureau members on watch.

Strangely enough, the most dramatic sighting of the summer was witnessed by two families who lived near the loch. Tom Thrush had just bought a new fiber-glass boat and decided to take his wife and daughter out for a short row. They had gone no more than fifty yards when they heard shouting. It was John and Ann Cameron from Inverness. "Look out!" they yelled. "Look out!"

The three Thrushes looked out, but there was nothing they could do. Two massive disturbances were heading in their general direction. One appeared to be approximately forty feet long; the other was somewhat shorter. It was Nessie and one of her playmates.

The people could only stare in horrified fascination as the ominous shapes moved in closer and closer. They reminded Tom Thrush of a pair of submarines. The two forms were only inches below the water's surface. When scarcely fifty yards away, a shiny, blackish-gray hump appeared above the smaller form. The creatures rushed past without giving anyone so much as a glance. Their wake caused so much turbulence, however, that the little boat was very nearly turned over.

For the rest of that summer, Tom Thrush had to row around Loch Ness by himself. Neither his wife nor his daughter was interested in his nice new boat. One short ride in it had been quite enough.

Less than a month before the Thrush family's harrowing experience, an English couple had watched Nessie at another game. Mr. and Mrs. Michael McLean were on the shore enjoying the afternoon sun when they saw a V-shaped something speeding toward them from the south. The object was churn-

133

ing up a tremendous wake. "What do you suppose that is?" McLean asked his wife.

Mrs. McLean ran to their car for the binoculars. At first glance, she thought that the thing might be an enormous duck. She knew, though, that this was impossible. A duck with a body thirty feet long just couldn't be true. Neither could a duck have its head sticking five or six feet above the water. There was only one thing that the creature could be. "I think," Mrs. McLean said slowly, "that we're seeing the Loch Ness Monster."

Her husband laughed and laughed and laughed. Then he asked his wife to let him have a look through the binoculars. Mrs. McLean refused to give them up. She was much too fascinated by what she was seeing. Besides, her husband often bragged about his excellent eyesight.

It looked to Mrs. McLean as though Nessie was playing some sort of monster game. She would rush madly in one direction, then suddenly change course. On two occasions, she sank straight down only to reappear a few seconds later. A number of times she surged partially out of the water and Mrs. McLean was able to see where the long neck swelled into a ridiculously large body.

Then a most remarkable thing occurred! A sea gull came skimming along above the surface of the loch. As it passed over Nessie's head, she made a mighty lunge at it. Her great body came so far out of the water that both of the observers were able to see a pair of flat paddlelike objects.

The flight of the gull marked the end of the game. Nessie shot off at top speed, then stopped suddenly, and sank like a rock.

When Mr. and Mrs. McLean went to bureau headquarters to report their sighting, the monster watchers almost burst into tears.

The sighting had taken place at a spot where a volunteer was normally stationed with binoculars and a camera with a powerful telephoto lens. On this particular afternoon, however, no one had manned the station. The noon weather report had predicted strong winds and heavy rain. Nessie didn't like that sort of weather, so the volunteers had stayed in camp. The weather report had been wrong, but by that time it had been too late to go out. Nessie, of course, hadn't heard the weather report and didn't know that she was supposed to have stayed at home.

People who come to bureau headquarters to report sighting are questioned closely. If two or more people have seen something unusual in the loch, each one is interrogated by a different member. He is also asked to fill in a form that lists thirty-six questions. The last step is to have him draw a rough sketch of whatever it was that he saw.

Less than half of the reports are accepted as valid. This doesn't mean that people are trying to play a trick on someone. Far from it. It simply means that many people honestly think that they have seen something that they actually have not seen at all.

There are a number of reasons for this. Tourists are so anxious to get a glimpse of the world-famous Loch Ness Monster that they're apt to mistake anything for Nessie. A log or a box or a boat might look like a monster if you really want to see a monster badly enough. Ripples and shadows on the water also confuse many people. So do the wakes of passing boats. The nature of Loch Ness is such that wakes can often be seen long after the boat has passed out of sight. Waves bouncing off the shore can easily be mistaken for a series of humps. Visitors see these and are absolutely convinced that they're seeing something entirely different. "There's Nessie!" they shout excitedly. "There's the Loch Ness Monster!"

Chapter **35**

The summers of 1969 and 1970 were times of frenzied activity at Loch Ness. Nessie, of course, was the cause of all this commotion. The search for the monster was being carried out on a truly large scale. "She won't escape us this time," the monster watchers promised one another.

It looked as though poor Nessie wouldn't have a chance. The odds didn't seem to be at all in her favor. Some of the most modern equipment on earth was lined up against her. The net appeared to be closing in.

Greater emphasis was now being placed on underwater exploration. Giant electronic corporations sent their technicians to Loch Ness, and several universities sent their electronics experts. Boats loaded with ultrasophisticated sounding devices floated silently around the loch. Sonar beams probed the depths and echo sounders aided the search.

Deep-sea divers also appeared on the scene, but they did not stay long. The high peat content in the water defeated them completely. At a depth of ten feet, they were barely able to distinguish large objects. When they reached a depth of thirty feet, they were no longer able to tell which way was up

An explorer and an electronics engineer discuss plans for the day's hunt for Nessie. The giant eel cage through which they are seen is being used in an attempt to catch one of the 11-foot-long eels reported to live in the Loch. It is part of one phase of the investigation to prove or disprove the theory that Nessie is some form of giant eel. (United Press International)

and which way was down. "This is the most frightening place I've ever dived," one diver confessed.

Two miniature submarines also got in on the act. The *Viper-Fish* was financed by Field Enterprises Educational Corporation of Chicago. Dan Taylor of Atlanta, Georgia, was the pilot. The *Pisces* was skippered by Captain Eastaugh and belonged to Vickers Corporation. It had been chartered by a film company, but the company permitted the captain to do independent research.

On his underwater journeys of exploration, Captain Eastaugh made some interesting discoveries. He first found a sunken sailing ship off Temple Pier. Although the ship was still in excellent condition, nobody knew where it had come from or for how long it had been there. Eastaugh also saw some white eels at a depth of over eight hundred feet. He learned, too, that the loch was much deeper than anyone had supposed. The maximum depth registered by sonar was nine hundred and seventy feet.

The *Viper-Fish* was a one-man mini-sub on loan to the Loch Ness Phenomena Investigation Bureau. If the sonar probes picked up any large diving creatures, Dan Taylor was supposed to go down in the mini-sub and give chase. But, alas! The poor little *Viper-Fish* simply couldn't cope with the inky-blackness and great depths of Loch Ness. Taylor had to be content with chugging back and forth at reasonable depths.

High above the mini-subs, the silently drifting boats, and the monster watchers on the shores, someone else was keeping an eye out for Nessie. This was Wing Commander Ken Wallis of the Royal Air Force. He was flying the tiny one-man autogyro that he had designed for a James Bond film. This time, though, the mini-helicopter was carrying aerial cameras instead of submachine guns.

Knowing that Nessie doesn't like noise, Wallis flew his

138

Dan Taylor of Atlanta, Georgia, searched for the Loch Ness Monster in a yellow mini-submarine donated by Field Enterprises Educational Corporation of Chicago.

little plane at an elevation of three thousand feet. By keeping the engine throttled as far back as possible, he was able to fly around with a minimum of sound.

Wallis was highly optimistic about his chances of spotting the monster. From his cockpit, he had a perfect view of the loch. Not only could he look in all directions, but he could also see any large object at a depth of ten feet or so beneath the surface. It only took him about twenty minutes to fly from one end of the loch to the other, so he was able to cover a lot of territory in a day of flying. When he spotted the monster, he would simply drop down and start snapping pictures.

139

The plan was a good one, but it lacked one very important thing. That one thing was Nessie's cooperation. Wallis flew back and forth until he was blue in the face. "I've got a feeling that Nessie is hiding away in a cavern somewhere and just laughing her head off," grumbled the pilot.

The days passed quickly. The autogyro, the mini-subs, the drifting boats, the electronics experts, and the monster watchers stayed on the job, but there was very little action. Enthusiasm and morale were beginning to sag when a most extraordinary thing happened!

Vincent Mulchrone, a reporter for the *Daily Mail,* had come to Loch Ness to do a series of articles on the monster. He had been there only a few days when he was approached by three young men from Yorkshire. They told the reporter that they had unearthed an enormous bone on the shore of the loch.

Mulchrone was understandably excited. He immediately alerted David James who came rushing over at once. The reporter and the member of Parliament accompanied the three Yorkshiremen to a spot on the shore and there lay the most massive bone they had ever seen.

The newspaperman was practically jumping for joy. This was the kind of story reporters dreamed of getting. He had certainly stumbled across the story of the year. Perhaps even the story of the century! This bone would prove beyond the shadow of a doubt that there were monsters in Loch Ness.

While Mulchrone photographed the massive bone from every angle, David James kept a discreet silence. It was a very interesting bone, but he wanted nothing to do with it. He believed that not even the largest creature in the loch could possibly possess a bone that size.

The world press delightedly gobbled up Mulchrone's story and pictures. Photos of the director of the Loch Ness

A camouflaged boat with cameras and echo-sounding equipment drifts silently about in search of Nessie.

Phenomena Investigation Bureau and the big bone appeared on the front pages of newspapers everywhere. Imaginations ran wild. A bone like that could only have come from a creature a hundred or more feet long, people said. The three young men from Yorkshire had made one of the most amazing discoveries of the century. They had proved that the Loch Ness Monster was one of the most monstrous monsters imaginable.

One of the men who was particularly interested in the big bone was the curator of the museum in Yorkshire. After studying the picture carefully, he phoned the police in Inverness. He had the skeleton of a large blue whale in his museum, he explained, and someone had recently stolen a part of its lower jawbone. The stolen bone, the curator continued, was an enormous thing. It was, in fact, the same size as the

141

bone found at Loch Ness by the three young men from York-shire.

Mulchrone was not one bit amused. He had been completely taken in and he didn't like it. The young men from Yorkshire had disappeared and so had the big bone. There was no one else to take his ill will out on, so he attacked Nessie. His story made a big splash on the front page of the *Daily Mail*. THE LOCH NESS MONSTER DOES NOT EXIST, declared the headline. The subheading stated that NESSIE IS A MYTH, A DELUSION, A TOURIST BAIT AND A FRAUD.

The article had only one significant effect. It made the scientists and monster watchers more determined than ever to find Nessie.

Chapter 36

Tourists who visited the Scottish Highlands during the summer of 1969 had a big surprise in store for them. They saw the Loch Ness Monster tied up at Temple Pier.

People stared and stared. They could hardly believe their eyes. Yet there she was and she was even larger than they had imagined. She was so large, in fact, that dozens of men were crawling all over her.

Nessie II had been built by technicians from London's Pinewood Studio. The film company had come to Loch Ness to shoot a mystery movie called *The Secret Lives of Sherlock Holmes*. Just what this great detective had to do with the Loch Ness Monster is as great a mystery as Nessie herself.

At any rate, a monster was needed for the film. Nessie, as usual, was being shy, so the film company built a model monster. It was some model! The enormous and ingenious affair was powered and controlled by batteries, transistors, and everything else the technicians could dream up. Although it was a very impressive monster indeed, the volunteer monster watchers from the Loch Ness Phenomena Investigation Bureau hated the thing.

The day finally came when Nessie II was all ready for her trial run. A large crowd was on hand to watch her maiden voyage. *Pisces,* one of the mini-subs, hooked onto her and off they went. It was a spectacular sight, but it didn't last long. Not more than five minutes after being launched, tragedy struck! Poor Nessie II gave a couple of feeble transistorized burps, then rolled over and sank in six hundred feet of water.

It was an emotional moment. The film directors wept monstrous tears and roared with anger. The technicians who had built the ill-fated monster hung their heads. Monster watchers from the Loch Ness Phenomena Investigation Bureau, however, couldn't stop laughing.

Other film units were also at the loch at that time. A British television company was filming *Legend of the Loch* and Walt Disney Studios was shooting a documentary. Both of the units were greatly interested in the activities of the Loch Ness Phenomena Investigation Bureau and the other expeditions that were searching for Nessie.

Although Nessie was sighted only fourteen times during the summer of 1969, there were some moments of intense excitement. Two fishermen named William Simpson and Duncan McDonell had a few moments that were so exciting they'll never be able to forget them.

The two young men were returning home from a fishing trip. It was a beautiful evening in late August and their cabin cruiser was cutting through the water at a leisurely pace. Suddenly, an enormous creature broke through the surface immediately in front of them! There was not enough time to swing out of its path. They struck the creature a glancing blow with the side of their boat.

Simpson immediately dashed into the cabin to turn off the gas. The collision had knocked a kettle off the stove and

144

Film technicians lower a model of the monster into the dark, choppy waters of Loch Ness.

he was afraid of an explosion. Then he remembered that he had a .22-caliber rifle on board. He was making a frantic search for it when he heard McDonell shouting for help.

A strange and frightening sight greeted Simpson when he charged back out onto the deck. His partner was trying to drive the monster away with an oar. The blade of the oar had been snapped off and McDonell was now jabbing at its throat with the broken shaft. Simpson swung into immediate action. He slammed the rifle against his shoulder and fired at point-blank range. The enormous creature dived immediately and disappeared in a flurry of foam.

145

A few hours after his horrifying experience, William Simpson was questioned closely by David James and Dr. Roy Mackal from the University of Chicago. Duncan McDonell, a truck driver, had already left for Glasgow, where he was interviewed by the British Broadcasting Corporation.

James and Mackal listened to the men's stories. They were identical in every way. It was also obvious that they had both had a very bad fright indeed. There seemed to be no reason to doubt their word. Neither one was at all interested in attracting attention to himself. Simpson, in fact, had told the story only to his uncle. It was the uncle who had then contacted David James.

The mystery of the monster was now more confusing than ever. Why, the scientists wondered, would a creature who disliked noise suddenly surface directly in the path of a power-driven boat? And why would it suddenly decide to attack?

But there was something even more mysterious about this incident. The two men had not been cruising on Loch Ness when they were attacked by the monster. They had been attacked by the monster while cruising on Loch Morar.

And Loch Morar is nearly forty miles from Loch Ness!

What now? the scientists and monster watchers asked one another.

One thing was perfectly clear. Nessie had never been to Loch Morar in her life. She was quite happy in her own loch and she certainly wouldn't go on a cross-country hike just to take a swim in another one. The monster in Loch Morar, therefore, could not possibly be the world-famous Loch Ness Monster. It had to be something else.

An investigation turned up some interesting bits of information. There *was* a monster in Loch Morar and her name was Morar Maggie. She had been seen quite a few times and

146

had been in the loch for as long as anyone could remember. According to eyewitness reports, Maggie and Nessie could have been twins.

But why didn't Morar Maggie ever get *her* name in the papers? people asked. Before her attack on the two fishermen, hardly anyone had ever heard of her. How did that happen?

This had once been true in Nessie's case as well. Her name had never appeared in the newspapers until work had begun on the new road along the loch. She had been seen many times, but word had not reached the outside world. Although most of the people living on the loch knew about Nessie, they weren't anxious to discuss her with a stranger.

Loch Morar is far more isolated today than Loch Ness was before the new road was built in the 1930's. Gaelic is still spoken in the Loch Morar region. Time has passed them by and little has changed over the ages. The people are friendly, but strangers are regarded with a degree of suspicion. There is no road along the loch, and the tiny village of Morar is no more than a cluster of houses. Mail is delivered only once a week. There is no hotel in the village and tourists are seldom seen.

The people living around Loch Ness are very fond of their monster. This is not true of the people at Loch Morar. They're inclined to be a bit superstitious. Old-timers, especially, look upon Morar Maggie as bad news. Some of them still believe that a member of the Gillie or McDonell families will die soon after the monster has been sighted.

In view of all this, it's not surprising that very few reports of Morar Maggie reached the outside world. She was a creature that the local people generally preferred not to discuss.

Like Loch Ness, Loch Morar is also an enormously deep loch and was once an arm of the sea. Both of the lochs were cut off from the sea at the end of the Ice Age. Loch Morar, however, is only a few feet above sea level and is much closer to the sea than Loch Ness. A monster in good condition could walk out of Loch Morar and be in the Atlantic Ocean five minutes later.

It's interesting to note here that it was in this immediate area that Dr. Matheson and his wife saw a strange beast that resembled a gigantic lizard. At that time, of course, Morar Maggie still hadn't had her name in the newspapers.

Chapter 37

Like it or not, the scientists and monster watchers now had another monster on their hands. An expedition spent part of the summer of 1970 at Loch Morar. The overwhelming bulk of activity, however, was carried on at Loch Ness.

Interest in Nessie had reached dizzying heights. Each year, the *Encyclopaedia Britannica* lists the ten subjects of greatest public interest. The list is drawn up on the basis of inquiries received from all parts of the world. To nobody's surprise, the Loch Ness Monster was high up on the list. It shared almost equal billing with such things as crimes of violence, the landing on the moon, and pollution. When Nessie was discussed in the House of Lords, parts of certain speeches were broadcast to the crew of Apollo 11.

Just imagine! Americans whizzing through space on a historic voyage to the moon were sent news of a prehistoric monster in a Scottish loch.

Most of the inquiries received about the Loch Ness Monster by the *Encyclopaedia Britannica* asked what kind of an animal Nessie was. Scientists and other interested people had been asking themselves this question for years. They were no

149

closer to the answer now than they were when the Surgeon's Photograph was published in 1934.

Although there were still people who said, "There ain't no such an animal," most scientists agreed that there was a huge unidentified creature of some type in Loch Ness. But what kind of a creature? Some sidestepped the issue by saying that it was a creature unknown to science. Others had their own pet theory.

Dr. Bernard Heuvelmans, a Dutch scientist, is a noted authority on giant sea serpents. Science, of course, says that these things do not exist, so Dr. Heuvelmans's position is truly unique. Nevertheless, the doctor has collected and analyzed reports of nearly four hundred sightings from all parts of the world. He concludes that forty-eight of the sightings referred to creatures remarkably similar to those described in Loch Ness.

It took a certain amount of courage to put forth this theory. Dr. Heuvelmans knows perfectly well that science refuses to admit the existence of giant sea serpents. He knows, too, that some scientists refuse to admit the existence of a monster in a Scottish loch. The doctor is actually saying, then, that something that is not supposed to exist is remarkably similar to something else that is not supposed to exist. These are brave words.

Dr. Roy Mackal, the University of Chicago professor, says, "We don't know whether the animals are air-breathers or non-air-breathers. If we're talking about air-breathers, my best bet would be a variety of sirenian, perhaps related to the manatee or sea cow. An Arctic sea cow, now thought to be extinct, did once exist."

Then the professor adds, "And, of course, there is always the possibility that we have here animals of a type simply unknown to us."

150

Mr. F. W. Holiday thinks that the Loch Ness Monster might be a worm. Yes, that's right. A worm. He's not referring, of course, to the kind of worm that boys dig up in their garden to catch fish with. Neither is he referring to "the dreadful beast, the direful wurrum—half fish and half dragon—that still survives in a mountain loch." He is referring to a fossil called *Tullimonstrum gregarium,* which is the Latin name for the Tully Monster.

In July, 1966, a monthly bulletin published by Chicago's Field Museum of Natural History featured an article and photographs by Dr. E. L. Richardson, Curator of Invertebrate Fossils. Dr. Richardson had been given a most unusual type of fossil. It was so unusual that he was unable to classify it. The thing just didn't seem to fit in anywhere. It was defying all the orderly rules of science. It was a freak and it had no right to exist.

Holiday read the article and studied the photographs. They showed a segmented, wormlike invertebrate. There was a tiny head, a slender, swan-type neck, and a long, torpedo-shaped body ending in a powerful tail. "That thing," Holiday exclaimed, "just might be the Loch Ness Monster!"

Dr. Richardson could neither agree nor disagree because his fossil stubbornly refused to let itself be classified. It was the most weird creature imaginable. The neck was flexible, but the head didn't seem to be a head. It was more like a claw armed with eight sharp teeth. The claw was most likely used for grasping food and here another problem popped up. Dr. Richardson couldn't find the creature's mouth.

There were other mysteries as well. The Tully Monster had sort of a barlike affair across its chest. At each end of the bar was a small organ shaped somewhat like a slice of tomato. There were a couple of tiny black dots on the organs and the scientist thought that these might be eyes. But were they?

151

Well, he couldn't be sure. He thought, too, that the round organs might also serve as a sonar device for swimming in murky water. Unfortunately, he couldn't be sure of that, either. Dr. Richardson was getting to hate the Tully Monster.

Holiday, though, thought that the Tully Monster was a very fine fellow indeed. He had managed to get a good look at Nessie and he felt that the two monsters might be cousins. Not everyone agrees with him, but no one has disproved his theory. Even his statement that the Loch Ness Monster may be a hundred feet long has not been seriously challenged.

One of the men who favors the plesiosaur theory is Tim Dinsdale. Tim has put in more time looking for Nessie than has anyone else. He can be seen at Loch Ness any summer and he's always doing the same thing. He's always drifting serenely around in his boat waiting for Nessie to pop up and say hello. Ironically, Dinsdale shot some movie film of the monster on his first trip to Loch Ness in 1960. He has returned to the loch for a few weeks each summer since, but his luck seems to have run out.

The theory that the Loch Ness Monster might be a plesiosaur is the most popular of all. "I prefer the plesiosaur theory because I *want* to prefer it," says Tim Dinsdale. This may not be very scientific, but it's easily understandable. It's terribly exciting to think that an enormous prehistoric seagoing dinosaur might be splashing around in a Scottish loch in the twentieth century.

If any man can be called an authority on the elusive Loch Ness Monster, that man would undoubtedly be Tim Dinsdale. He caught monster fever in 1960 and has suffered from it ever since. When he isn't actually looking for Nessie, he's thinking about her.

Hundreds of eyewitnesses have been interviewed by him. A surprisingly large number of them have described a crea-

152

ture that *could* be a plesiosaur. Dinsdale cheerfully admits that he wants Nessie to be a prehistoric monster, but he goes one step further. "If the Loch Ness Monster is *not* a plesiosaur," he says, "then it is a type of animal completely unknown to science."

David James, founder of the Loch Ness Phenomena Investigation Bureau, has been directing the search for Nessie since 1962. He is the man who first kicked things off on a really grand scale. James was instrumental in bringing the mini-sub, the mini-helicopter, the electronics experts, the volunteer monster watchers, and a host of other people to the loch. No man has done more to put the Loch Ness Monster on the map. The single sad note in all this is that James himself has never seen the monster.

This is somewhat of a disappointment, of course, but he is still optimistic. The electronics people have charted "huge, obviously animate creatures" on their sonar screens. Monster watchers have reported quite a few sightings and have shot some film of unidentified creatures. Reports from tourists and local inhabitants drift into bureau headquarters every once in a while. The end of the search could come at any moment.

"One of these days," predicts David James, "the right man with the right camera will be in the right place at the right time."

When that day comes, the world's most baffling, intriguing, and amusing mystery—The Mystery of the Loch Ness Monster—will at last be solved.

Elwood D. Baumann was born in Saskatchewan, Canada, and is a graduate of the University of Wisconsin. After many years as a teacher and principal in schools in Venezuela and eastern Turkey, he took up writing as a vocation and travel as an avocation and has now been in one hundred and five countries on six continents.

Mr. Baumann has spent the last two summers in the Scottish Highlands and knows Loch Ness well. Like other visitors, he became intrigued by the mystery of the monster. He learned that everyone had heard of Nessie but very few people knew anything at all about her. It was then that he began to gather material for this story of the search for the world's most famous monster.

The author is a member of The Loch Ness Phenomena Investigation Bureau and is now living in Ross and Cromarty, Scotland.